Praise for *Diversity Beyond Lip Service*

"*Diversity Beyond Lip Service* makes a good read for all concerned with the question of human training, leadership development, and organizational change. It challenges us to think about diversity in more concrete ways to ensure transformative change in organizational leadership and within institutional structures. At the heart of diversity is addressing the power and structural issues of critical engagement of ideas, beliefs, practices, and social action. The book's major strength is the focus on concrete and actionable practices to realize the hopes and dreams of genuine inclusion and diversity."
—**George J. Sefa Dei, Professor of Social Justice Education,**
 Ontario Institute for Studies in Education, University of Toronto,
 and Fellow, Royal Society of Canada

"*Diversity Beyond Lip Service: A Coaching Guide for Challenging Bias* provides a clear, powerful guide through what a growing number of us in the coaching profession believe is imperative to our survival and relevance as a profession. To provide the service to our clients that we claim, we must do our own work to become aware of our personal and organizational blind spots and biases in the complex realm of diversity and inclusion. Through many powerful examples, and with a very calm, incontrovertible voice, La'Wana Harris has made the intersection between coaching and inclusion work crystal clear. Bravo!"
—**Halli MacNab, PCC, President, Association of Coach Training Organizations,**
 and Chief Operating Officer, Accomplishment Coaching

"La'Wana Harris has opened this coach's eyes to the power of coaching practices to create new paths for diversity and inclusion work—whether or not you are formally trained as a coach. Please read this book and help create workplaces with honest engagement and access for all."
—**Marshall Goldsmith, Thinkers50 #1 Executive Coach and**
 two-time #1 Leadership Thinker in the World

"*Diversity Beyond Lip Service* is a wonderful guide to diversity and inclusion for intelligent, caring human beings and their organizations. La'Wana Harris wants us to understand that inclusivity is *everyone's* responsibility. There's no shaming or finger-pointing here. We all have room to improve—because whether we know it or not, we all have biases. No matter who you are, you'll be a better person for reading this book."
—**Ken Blanchard, coauthor of *The New One Minute Manager*® and**
 Servant Leadership in Action

"Coaching is about expanding people's view of themselves and the world around them. La'Wana Harris demonstrates how we can use a coaching approach in conversations to help people courageously recognize when they have acted out of judgment, power, and privilege. We don't need to be told to be more inclusive; we need people who help make awareness and inclusion a conscious choice, even when the conversations feel uncomfortable. All leaders, coaches, and people who care about healing the divisiveness in the workplace and the world should practice what they learn from this book."

—**Marcia Reynolds, board member and past Global President,
  International Coach Federation, and author of** *The Discomfort Zone*

DIVERSITY
BEYOND
LIP SERVICE

DIVERSITY
BEYOND
LIP SERVICE

A **COACHING GUIDE** FOR **CHALLENGING BIAS**

LA'WANA HARRIS

Berrett–Koehler Publishers, Inc.

Berrett-Koehler Publishers, Inc.
1333 Broadway, Suite 1000
Oakland, CA 94612-1921
Tel: (510) 817-2277
Fax: (510) 817-2278
www.bkconnection.com

ORDERING INFORMATION

Quantity sales. Special discounts are available on quantity purchases by corporations, associations, and others. For details, contact the "Special Sales Department" at the Berrett-Koehler address above.

Individual sales. Berrett-Koehler publications are available through most bookstores. They can also be ordered directly from Berrett-Koehler: Tel: (800) 929-2929; Fax: (802) 864-7626; www.bkconnection.com.

Orders for college textbook / course adoption use. Please contact Berrett-Koehler: Tel: (800) 929-2929; Fax: (802) 864-7626.

Distributed to the U.S. trade and internationally by Penguin Random House Publisher Services.

Berrett-Koehler and the BK logo are registered trademarks of Berrett-Koehler Publishers, Inc.

Printed in Canada

Berrett-Koehler books are printed on long-lasting acid-free paper. When it is available, we choose paper that has been manufactured by environmentally responsible processes. These may include using trees grown in sustainable forests, incorporating recycled paper, minimizing chlorine in bleaching, or recycling the energy produced at the paper mill.

Library of Congress Cataloging-in-Publication Data
Name: Harris, La'Wana, author.
    Title: Diversity beyond lip service : a coaching guide for challenging bias / La'Wana Harris.
    Description: First edition. | Oakland, CA : Berrett-Koehler Publishers, Inc., [2019] | Includes bibliographical references and index.
    Identifiers: LCCN 2018053555 | ISBN 9781523098675 (pbk.)
    Subjects: LCSH: Diversity in the workplace. | Minorities--Employment. | Executive coaching. | Employees--Coaching of.
    Classification: LCC HF5549.5.M5 H36735 2018 | DDC 658.3008--dc23
    LC record available at https://lccn.loc.gov/2018053555

First Edition
27 26 25 24 23 22 21 20 19   10 9 8 7 6 5 4 3 2 1

Book producer: Linda Jupiter Productions
Editor: Elissa Rabellino
Text designer: Morning Hullinger, The Color Mill

Cover designer: Paula Goldstein
Proofreader: Mary Kanable
Indexer: Paula C. Durbin-Westby

*This book is dedicated to
my grandmother Mildred, who taught me that
a life well spent is one that was lived
in service to others.*

CONTENTS

FOREWORD

I first met La'Wana after I reached out to meet her. I contacted her because I saw what she did and I was impressed. I wanted to hear a bit more about her coaching, and about her experience as a diversity and inclusion expert. We met very soon afterward while I was speaking at an event, and La'Wana happened to be the moderator assigned to introduce me and to facilitate questions after my session. Within a very short time of meeting her, I knew that I had a lot to learn from La'Wana. When she asked me to write the foreword for her book, *Diversity Beyond Lip Service*, at first I was humbled, then I was nervous! But as La'Wana might coach, I'll tell my truth.

Part of the goal of a foreword is to tell you what you're likely to get out of reading the book. I'm not going to do that. I won't tell you what you're liable to get out of this; in some ways, that would fly in the face of everything this book is about. Instead, I'll tell you what I got out of it. Because a guide that is focused on how to be authentic and be a better coach, leader, and in many ways a better individual deserves no less than some genuine reflection and truth-telling.

What I got out of *Diversity Beyond Lip Service* was a set of resources. There are relevant models that will help me as I continue to reflect on my personal journey and how I show up in the world as a father of two interracial sons—one already a man, a sophomore at Duke, and the other a precocious eight-year-old. La'Wana's words about how we choose to embrace, or hide from, our role in pursuing diversity, equity, inclusion, and belonging will undoubtedly resonate with me for a long time. I also got a good helping of anecdotes and stories—some that spoke to me as if I could have been the person writing the words, others that mirror experiences I've had during my time in business, and a few that were new and unique. These anecdotes are real, genuine, and heartfelt, and they add a humanity that gives the book warmth and approachability.

I don't agree with everything La'Wana wrote. And in many ways, I think that's exactly how she'd want it. La'Wana provides her point of view—an educated, personal, and experienced point of view—but she doesn't try to convince the reader. Rather, she takes us on a journey of discovery and reflection and allows us to make up our own mind. She introduces us to conflict and pushes us to take a side. She is bold in her statements and powerful in her confidence, and through her prose she encourages us to be the same. I can think of no better way to honor the truth of her writing than to sometimes vociferously disagree, sometimes intently concur, and other times simply read, learn, and reflect; to see the world through eyes that are not my own and borrow her perspective on business, coaching, inclusion, and, more broadly, life. *Diversity Beyond Lip Service* defies being just one thing and instead is a guide, a resource, a set of tools, and a journal of the experience of a leader in coaching and corporate leadership.

That's my truth—now go find yours.

Khalil Smith
Head of Diversity and Inclusion Practice
NeuroLeadership Institute

PREFACE

As a coach specializing in DEIB (diversity, equity, inclusion, and belonging) with decades of experience in corporate organizations, I understand the pervasive and limiting effects of less-than-optimal diversity and inclusion practices—what I call D&I lip service. I know firsthand how the superficial expression of support for a diverse and inclusive culture without any corresponding action or sincere intent to effect meaningful change can hinder companies' talent acquisition, retention, and—perhaps above all—bottom lines.

You can be sure that I've seen it all. I've encouraged executives to set the standard for diversity practices and watched them reap the corresponding benefits. I've talked teams through tough conversations that helped them turn their ships toward better D&I policies and processes and corresponding boosts in revenue. And I've looked on as leaders refused to acknowledge their biases and systematically dismantled their own organizations as a result, businesses that could have thrived with a broader approach and input from a diversity of voices. I've included voices of diversity throughout the book to help show the tremendous value that diverse perspectives bring to business and society as a whole. I know that D&I efforts make a difference.

My impetus for addressing the importance of inclusion and how to create it in the workplace also comes from myriad of personal experiences—some good and some less so. On the positive side, I still have vivid memories of my first formal diversity and inclusion training almost twenty years ago with the Center for Creative Leadership and the Greensboro Chamber of Commerce. At that time, I was introduced to Other Voices and Leadership Greensboro, two leadership-development programs that helped fuel my passion for social justice and shaped the diversity-and-inclusion-focused professional I am today.

Other Voices is a nine-month leadership-development and community-building program that seeks to examine the many forms diversity takes and to understand the roots and impact of prejudice and oppression. During an eye-opening nine months, I gained a more holistic understanding of how power, privilege, bias, and prejudice work, and simultaneously engaged in the process of transforming my own culturally absorbed biases.

The Leadership Greensboro program is focused on empowering a diverse group of people in Greensboro, North Carolina, to become responsible leaders in business, education, community and civic organizations, government, and neighborhood action. During these programs, I embraced the leadership-and-community-building model and, along with the other participants, developed pragmatic skills for working with diverse groups for collective action.

On the negative side, as an African-American woman living in the South and working in the corporate world, I have experienced the ugliness of discrimination and prejudice firsthand—a reality that is all too common for many who are considered "different" by virtue of their race, gender, ethnicity, religious affiliation, sexual orientation, disability, age, or socioeconomic status. Suffice it to say that I do not want anyone else to experience the kind of debilitating and disempowering treatment that I have endured inside and outside of the workplace.

When I reflect on times throughout history that have been plagued by overt and systemic racism, prejudice, and privilege, I remember the saying, "If you want to know what you would have done back then, take a look at what you are doing right now."

I hope that as an African-American back then, I would have sat on the buses and marched in the streets during the civil rights movement, or even run away to secure my freedom during slavery. But the reality is that I am alive right now, and there is still important work to do for the advancement of justice and equality for all. To make a difference, all I can do is focus on changing the present. This book is my contribution to progress.

And while I'd like to say that my work is solely altruistic, my desire to see momentous progress made in diversity, equity, and inclusion in my lifetime is also fueled by my grandson, whom I love dearly and would like to protect from all forms of senseless injustice. I aim to help reshape the world so that he and others like him have the same opportunity to use their gifts and abilities to succeed as those who are not perceived as "different" have long enjoyed.

I don't have all the answers, but I will be part of the solution by offering what I've learned about creating inclusion in both the for-profit and nonprofit sectors, with the hope that change will arrive more easily and swiftly for the next generation.

The case has long been made for D&I. Our heads are convinced. What we need to do now is work on our hearts to get them in the right, welcoming place and then use our hands to start creating change. My heart-and-hands approach is based on provoking meaningful and often uncomfortable self-reflection and brutally honest conversations that lead to courageous action. It is the hard, awkward, and necessary work that needs to be done toward establishing environments in which every individual is committed to being an agent of change within their sphere of influence. It is how we move beyond D&I lip service.

Diversity and Inclusion Starts from Within

◆ *We've been talking about diversity and inclusion for decades.*

◆ *Why aren't we further along?*

◆ *What's really going on?*

This book is written for the power construct within your organization (let's face it, mostly white men).

As a woman of color, I don't know what it feels like to be at the top of the power structure and look to the left and right and see only people who look like me. I also don't know what it feels like to be a member of the majority who is bombarded with messages, perhaps for the first time in a decades-long career, stating that my utopia is really an oasis that is no longer good for business. However, I want to understand your experience without condemning and judging. I believe it's important to have compassion and empathy for all people involved in diversity and inclusion. And on a more pragmatic level, you are the people who hold the power and the purse strings: If you aren't engaged on a deeper level, we will not see results.

I believe that as a society we have to start where we are. And so, together, let us tackle some of the tough questions that have been avoided in the mainstream narrative, such as:

◆ *How do we recognize that for some members of the majority, replacing their colleagues with women, people of color, and other underrepresented groups makes them uncomfortable?*

Let us acknowledge and move forward from the truth that this discomfort fuels an unspoken fear that advancing D&I means you may lose some of your power. Said differently, let us begin from a place of understanding that to those who are accustomed to privilege, equality can feel like oppression.

But this is not about my letting anyone off the hook. I firmly believe that members of the majority must move beyond passive support on the fringe to proactively using their privilege to benefit everyone. I just know that we won't get there without a healthy dose of empathy and understanding about what it will take for you, the people in power, to feel good about sharing it.

COACHING + D&I = Δ BEHAVIOR

Collectively, we can assist with this process by creating a judgment-free environment where majority group leaders are encouraged to explore their role in the power construct. Removing judgment and blame helps establish a foundation we can build upon in order to reframe the role of privilege as a platform to share power, and to ensure that all people are valued and respected and that all voices are heard.

We can choose to completely turn privilege on its head by transforming what has historically served as a barrier into an enabler of inclusivity—but it will require a fundamental shift in how we approach D&I.

Traditional efforts have been oriented from the "outside in." We've spent decades telling people what they should think, say, and do relative to inclusivity. I'm proposing an "inside out" coaching approach that encourages individuals to go deep within to own where they are, embrace radical truth, and do the self-work needed to progress along their diversity and inclusion journey.

It is from this precipice that I introduce a new inclusion model and a coaching platform—Inclusion Coaching—based on the most up-to-date research and best practices for creating sustainable and meaningful behavioral change. I also provide an action-oriented process—COMMIT—with simple techniques to shift mind-sets and encourage more inclusive behaviors.

Commit to Courageous Action

Open Your Eyes and Ears

Move beyond Lip Service

Make Room for Controversy and Conflict

Invite New Perspectives

Tell the Truth Even When It Hurts

By introducing a new approach at the intersection of coaching and D&I, I am offering your organization a viable solution for the "how" of everyday inclusion.

Using the tenets and principles of professional coaching, we can get beneath the superficial layers of engagement by shifting the focus away from *telling* and *persuading* toward *asking* the right questions and *listening*. We can create a space for self-reflection at the level of a person's core values, beliefs, and motivators to find what they need in order to embrace inclusion versus being pushed to simply comply. Because, honestly, the latter will only take you to the point of lip service. It's time to move beyond.

IN THIS BOOK

In the first chapter of this book, I outline the problem with most D&I initiatives and why so many never go beyond lip service—for example, working diligently to hire diverse employees but not being able to retain them past one year. The second chapter is about the language of diversity. By naming the concepts and the ways in which different groups are marginalized, we begin to create more awareness of the workplace practices that unwittingly foster bias, privilege, and discrimination so that we can more fully explore why we hold on to them.

Chapter 3 goes deep into the problem and power of privilege, a critical concept in moving beyond diversity and inclusion lip service. I explore why D&I is hard for the people in power and how we can work empathetically with them to dismantle their resistance and coach them in becoming champions for a more inclusive environment.

In chapter 4, I explain why coaching is the most effective model for behavior change (short explanation: it encourages people to ask important questions of themselves and play a vital part in their own understanding of D&I and its value). I also explain how the COMMIT coaching model can support individuals in moving beyond D&I lip service with clear guidelines for building a mind-set and environment where inclusion can thrive.

While the six steps sound (and are) simple, they are not necessarily easy. That is why I devote each of the next six chapters to exploring one step of the COMMIT process. Then, just as I coach others on facing their truths, I tell my own in chapter 11 as a model for owning your own stories.

Because creating inclusive cultures requires that everyone be on board, throughout the book I will show how you can do your part to ensure that all voices are heard and valued in your organization's conversation—regardless of where you fall in the power structure. Former clients, contributors, and colleagues have graciously lent their voices and insights to the discussion, although names and companies have been changed for those who prefer to remain anonymous. The application tools throughout the book will also help you take steps toward increasing inclusion at your organization and in your life. You can visit lawanaharris.com for additional information and resources.

A PATH FORWARD TOGETHER

My life experiences as an African-American woman compel me to do all that I can to advance diversity and inclusion in the workplace, especially as I face the harsh reality that I likely have more years behind me than ahead of me. With almost three decades of civic activism and two decades of corporate experience with large multinational organizations, I've experienced the good, the bad, and the ugly. It's time to pay it forward by sharing the triumphs, failures, and lessons learned to help others coming along in the next generation of leaders.

And so, instead of beginning to plan for a graceful exit, I'd rather shake things up a bit and leverage my experience as a Certified Diversity Executive, an International Coach Federation Certified Coach, and a global leadership development professional to offer solutions to improve your overall effectiveness as an individual, provide support to your internal diversity and inclusion function, and share tangible means to reform the exclusionary behaviors and various negative "isms" felt by many within your organization.

We are all at different places along our journeys, some further along than others. We need to put our own biases aside and give the people making the decisions about D&I the space to understand their truths when it comes to the topic, their privilege, and *how* they feel about all of these factors, without telling them how they *should* feel. From that point of self-actualization, vulnerability, and humility, we can build a path forward—together.

It's time to face the unspoken truths and deal with whatever shows up.

CHAPTER 1

We Hired Some Minorities, Some Women, and People with Disabilities; Isn't That Enough?

*Increasing diversity without increasing inclusion
is a recipe for failure.*

When Vanessa Robbins was hired by the Atlanta office of regional corporation Setco, she was excited that her new "assistant director of brand development" position not only was a good professional opportunity but also seemed like the right next step in her marketing career.

Ambitious and a hard worker, Vanessa had high hopes for where her professional pathway might lead—partly because in her previous position with a smaller company, she was repeatedly recognized for her outstanding creativity and ability to grasp any problem quickly. It was nice to feel valued by her employer, but it wasn't such a big deal, given that she'd graduated from an Ivy

League university, and, not coincidentally, both of her parents were physicians. She wasn't blind to the fact that she possessed the right credentials for success in corporate America, in addition to her demonstrated abilities, which had also been well acknowledged during her college years.

For their part, the human resources department and senior-executive leadership team at Setco, who interviewed and ultimately hired Vanessa, an African-American woman, were pleased to move their firm's "diversity quotient" forward. The pressure they'd been facing from their board of directors was getting intense, and hiring Vanessa meant they could demonstrate progress in an area that they'd long neglected and, truth be told, simply was not a priority.

It wasn't as if they'd never read all those studies about diversity and inclusion helping companies gain a competitive edge; they just hoped the push toward a diverse workforce was one of those organizational-change fads that would take care of itself without any dedicated resources or attention. They liked the fact that everyone knew what to expect at Setco. Their organizational sentiment toward D&I could be summed up in a few statements: Things were stable, with the company pecking order well established and religiously followed. Besides, it's hard to even talk to people who aren't like you; they are just on a different page. The whole diversity thing was time-consuming and not worth the extra effort, as far as they were concerned.

But they had to do something. And now they had. Hiring Vanessa was the first big step toward a more diverse organization, and they hoped it would work. She was sufficient leadership-level "diversity," so the board could return to discussing the operational issues that senior leadership felt far more comfortable addressing.

REFLEXIVE MARGINALIZATION: MAINTAINING THE STATUS QUO

In her first three months at her new company, Vanessa noticed a pattern that bothered her and even caused her to lose sleep a few nights. More than once, she tried to rationalize away the stonewalling she felt whenever she offered her opinions or ideas, telling herself that perhaps she was mistaken. Was she still too new for people to know her name or listen to her suggestions? Whatever the reason, it wasn't what she expected or was used to experiencing.

In her last job, there had been a widely diverse workforce and an inclusive corporate culture. The senior leadership team was made up of a diverse demographic of executives that mirrored their employees and customer base. No one felt like an outsider or like they were marginalized because of their ethnicity, race, gender, or sexual identity. Simply put, discrimination hadn't been tolerated in any form—overtly or covertly. If it did occur, it was quickly addressed.

But Setco was different in this regard, and Vanessa was taken aback by that difference. During the extensive interview process, she'd been praised for her accomplishments and background and for her thoughtful, nuanced answers to the complex questions posed to her. The HR person even told her that several people at the firm saw her as the most qualified and promising candidate they had interviewed in a long time.

They brought me on to contribute at a high level, she reminded herself, thinking back on what was said during her onboarding meeting, *so that's exactly what I am going to do.*

Focusing on a solution, she came up with a plan. She would do observational research in order to figure out what was going on. At the next three team meetings, she carefully studied the group's dynamics: Carl directed the meetings, and Mike and John were usually the ones offering input, while the other woman on the team—who happened to be white—contributed only rarely. When she did say something, Carl would thank her and immediately turn to either Mike or John for their opinion.

"So, Mike," he'd say, "what do you think of Rita's observation?"

And Mike would reiterate what Rita had said and then talk around it until it became so buried under his verbiage that her input was long forgotten.

Oh, thought Vanessa, *it's a gender thing.* She decided to talk to Rita about the behavior she'd observed. But when Vanessa found a private moment to do that, Rita seemed resigned.

"Yeah, they're kind of old school here," she admitted. "But I hardly notice it anymore. You'll get used to it, too. They expect deference from women—but what else is new? Hey, it's a job," she added with a shrug. "It pays well, and I'm a single mother, so I can't afford to rock any boats. My kids and my mother depend on me. My dad died of a heart attack a year ago and my mom's living with us now."

Vanessa expressed concern, saying she could understand Rita's position. But as she walked away, Vanessa thought about the fact that this really wasn't what she had signed up for at Setco, and she felt it physically—as if she were now buried up to her neck in cement. Later that day, after recovering a bit, she decided to push back. There had to be a way to break through, not only for herself, but also for the betterment of her team and the organization as a whole.

Steeling herself at the next team meeting a few weeks later, Vanessa jotted down a few notes while Carl talked, preparing her response to what he was asking the team to brainstorm about. When he paused and looked at Mike and then John, she saw her chance.

"What about . . ." Vanessa began, and she laid out a three-point plan for a marketing campaign designed to launch Setco's new high-value product, which was what Carl had wanted the marketing team to address.

Everyone around the conference table turned to look at Vanessa in apparent disbelief. The facial expressions of the men transformed from uncomfortable to sullen, as if they couldn't quite figure out how to process the fact that she had confidently contributed such great, on-point ideas. But Rita, Vanessa could see, was struggling not to smile. Covering her mouth, she coughed several times and reached for her water bottle.

When Vanessa finished speaking, Carl stared out the window for a few weighty seconds before asking, "Anyone care to respond?"

John leaned forward slightly, as if he were about to speak but, thinking better of it, sat back in his chair and said nothing.

"All right, then," Carl said. "Let's move on."

Vanessa felt like she'd been punched in the stomach. This dismissal of her contribution was so blatant that for a good fifteen seconds, she considered walking out of the meeting and handing in her resignation as soon as she could type it up. Instead, she waited to calm down, and then it occurred to her that she could talk with her manager, Claire, someone who had a vested interest in her success at Setco.

The next day, which was a Friday, she arranged a meeting with Claire and spent a good hour preparing. She planned her approach with care, wanting to present her concerns without seeming too emotional. She even came up with a way that her manager could help her work things out with Carl and the team.

Vanessa began slowly, trying to outline her frustrating experiences during team meetings and conference calls in a way that wasn't too critical of the company while still sharing her disappointment at being marginalized, if not outright dismissed. Vanessa also talked about why she'd taken the job and how this apparent gender bias hadn't been clear during the interview process.

Claire pursed her lips tightly while Vanessa was speaking, looking ever more annoyed. Pausing just slightly, she asked if Vanessa thought she might be misreading her situation.

"Keep in mind," Claire added, "you are one of the very few African-Americans working at various levels in the company, and the only one at this level, so you may be a little sensitive . . . to certain things."

By now, Vanessa had guessed that Claire was invested in the company's unspoken marginalization strategy for those who weren't part of the preferred demographic. But something prompted Vanessa to try again. So she shared that ten minutes after the incident in which her plan for a product launch was oddly dismissed, John had mentioned a very similar approach, and Carl had pounced on it, calling it "brilliant thinking."

And, Vanessa continued, for weeks before this incident, John and a few others on her team had been asking her to meet privately with them to brainstorm because, they said, "You have great ideas." But then, at the next meeting, they would present her ideas as their own while she sat across from them in disbelief.

"Hmmm," said Claire. "Would you like to know what it sounds like to me?"

"Yes," replied Vanessa, though she doubted that Claire would present an objective perspective, given what she'd said earlier.

"It seems you haven't quite grasped the concept of being a team player, Vanessa. You're also sounding like a 'victim,' you know? Many women feel this way, and it's often because they aren't taking responsibility for themselves. In your case, that would mean your professional development. You need to think less about others' behavior and more about how you can alter your own. After all," she added, as if it were the most novel concept in the world, "you are the only person you can control."

Vanessa could see that Claire was prepared for some kind of pushback—perhaps her manager even realized that this platitude was, at the very least, missing the point—but she refused to give Claire the satisfaction of eliciting less-than-professional behavior. Instead, she offered a polite response to Claire's patronizing suggestion and found a graceful way to end the meeting.

This kind of exchange is all too common in many organizations that have hired diverse talent without creating an inclusive environment to retain and develop their new talent. Leaders in a noninclusive culture default to putting all impetus for change on the individual versus owning the impact of systemic processes and exclusionary behavioral patterns.

Once Vanessa was back at her desk, preparing to leave for the weekend, she thought to herself, *What am I going to do now?*

LIP SERVICE AND BEYOND

Before we get any deeper into our journey toward greater diversity, equity, and inclusion, let me define exactly what we are talking about. *Diversity* is the spectrum of human difference. *Equity* refers to equal opportunity for all humans—an environment free from bias, harassment, and discrimination. *Inclusion* empowers all people to access the same opportunities and challenges; to receive the same level of respect and value; and to be treated as they desire to be treated, regardless of inherent or perceived differences.

So, then, what is D&I lip service? Think of lip service as a company hiring one or two people of color and putting them on display on their website as if "diversity" has been achieved, much like in Vanessa's story.

Lip service is an "Everyone is welcomed here!" corporate declaration. There is intentionality about diversity in visual marketing, but the employee experience does not align with the words in the mission statement or the assortment of diverse smiling faces in the corporate presentation. This misalignment often shows up in the hemorrhaging of diverse talent (this is what eventually happened with Vanessa). They quickly exit the organization due to not feeling included or valued. For a company like Setco, going "beyond lip service" would start with engaging inclusion strategies before employees were even hired, such as connecting them with the appropriate internal employee resource groups, mentors, or other support and resources that would set them up for success.

Hiring professionals at large organizations often feel that they have done their job when they have brought in "diverse" talent, but there is a big difference between acquiring greater diversity and achieving true inclusion. Hiring to create diversity alone—checking off boxes on a corporate hiring profile by increasing the representation from a few target populations—is not a wise maneuver. Here's why:

Unless you're working toward real inclusiveness, you may find that within a year, an alarming number of those hires have left the organization. Their exit interviews may reveal additional clues about the limitations of diverse hiring strategies when there are not inclusive practices in place to support the engagement and success of all employees. And it's truly a lose–lose situation when new employees are hired and trained, only to leave the organization before realizing their potential for optimal performance.

☛ When employees cannot contribute in a manner they find fulfilling, they must set out in search of companies where they feel truly welcomed, valued, and rewarded, where their unique perspectives are exactly what the business is looking for and their insights are put to good use.

By the same token, companies that hire just to fill a quota waste time, effort, and—of course—funds preparing people for roles they won't fill long-term and searching for new talent when those individuals inevitably leave.

This is exactly what happened with Vanessa: After eight months of soul-searching and struggle, she decided to move on, and her next career move could not have been better for her. Hired as vice president of sales and marketing at Makeda, a major tech company, Vanessa feels empowered in her new role. She knows she can bring all her unique gifts and talents to bear while being her authentic self at a company that truly values what she has to offer.

So, how could this situation have been avoided? How can we reach true diversity and inclusion, rather than just paying lip service in the form of a few diverse hires? My next example will show you.

SVP GOODE GETS D&I RIGHT

This is a story about a white male senior vice president at a Fortune 500 firm who embodied everything about high "inclusion intelligence" that one could hope to see. This executive, whom I'll refer to by the pseudonym SVP Goode, came to the United States from Italy. He was uniquely gifted in the areas of emotional intelligence, compassion, and business savvy.

Working from his leadership level within the organization, he was able to institute a number of previously unimaginable initiatives to benefit women, people of color, and everyone else.

Goode began by hiring a woman of color as the corporation's head of global marketing—a move that was unprecedented at that level in the organization—and then he did much more.

He proactively recruited a diverse pool of talent for his leadership team and held them accountable for doing the same with their direct reports. He refused to accept the fallacy that it is hard to find top talent from different cultures, ethnicities, abilities, and genders. And when he did assemble a diverse team, Goode was very intentional in his efforts to reverse a trend seen in many large organizations, where employees are hired for individuality but rewarded for conformity. He quite deliberately celebrated and promoted what made each team member different—and therefore valuable to the organization—by asking for their perspective based on their unique experience, rather than trying to get them to think, act, and behave like everyone else.

Next, he held café-style meetings to get to know people by actually listening to them, as opposed to taking a traditional top-down approach, in which a leader is intent upon enlightening those at lower levels in the corporate hierarchy. By listening closely, he discovered what each person loved to do, and what he or she was especially good at doing. He then used this information to give that individual more flexibility in his or her job. If, for instance, someone was hired to work on external partnerships, but she was also a great creative designer, he encouraged her to use her additional skills as part of fluid project teams. These teams were assembled based on their members' talents, rather than their job titles or responsibilities.

This agile, talent-based model enabled people to bring all of their varied skills to work. In addition to having happy, productive employees, the company reaped a number of indirect benefits. For one, offering people that level of flexibility meant the company was maximizing internal capacity and discovering new skill sets within the existing workforce. As a result, they no longer needed to outsource certain jobs, creating significant cost savings.

Apart from those initiatives, Goode also offered development opportunities for everyone—not just a select few "high potentials," as is often the case. He advocated for all of his employees, understanding the importance of maximizing the potential of his most valuable resource: his people. And people loved working for him—so much so that his team had a very high retention score. Each person felt seen, heard, recognized, valued, challenged, and given the support to develop his or her professional abilities.

Even more astonishing, this SVP championed the needs of parents with small children by advocating for a robust and holistic family-leave policy, which included paid time off for both mothers and fathers. He even helped make it possible for women who were nursing to continue to do so while coming to work each day and while attending off-site meetings after he identified this need during one of his listening sessions. In the end, because of SVP Goode's many efforts, his organization received a number of diversity awards.

So what did this executive do right that others so often don't even consider? He used his influence to help transform his organization.

He understood that it wasn't enough to hire a handful of people who were members of typically disenfranchised groups just to meet an arbitrary quota for the sake of representation. Instead, after onboarding women and minorities into visible positions of responsibility, he supported them by listening to them and structuring their work and their work life around the whole of who they were. He did this to make it possible for them to contribute every bit of value they could bring to the table by virtue of being their authentic selves on the job, in addition to using their job-related skills, abilities, expertise, and experience.

TRANSFORM—DON'T CONFORM—FOR BUSINESS SUCCESS

If your company's motto is akin to "When in Rome . . . ," then Rome is likely about to fall—whether you know it or not.

According to the U.S. Census Bureau, by 2020, "More than half the nation's children are expected to be part of a minority race or ethnic group," and by 2060, just 36 percent of people under age eighteen will be single-race, non-Hispanic European-American, compared with 52 percent today. The U.S. population as a whole is expected to follow a similar trend, becoming majority-minority in 2044.[1] What the data so clearly indicate is that diverse groups will be writing the next chapter in every corporate narrative.

☛ Our understanding of how to attract and retain— and market to—an increasingly diverse and global demographic is virtually *the only way* to succeed going forward.

Continuing to thrive is a matter of embracing what is inevitable. That is why businesses must alter employee demographics so that they mirror customers' profiles. And since the days of enforcing a narrow standard for success are rapidly receding into the rearview, we must also build inclusive corporate cultures to support our new heterogenous makeups.

Anyone can conform to his or her organization. I'm challenging you to look for opportunities to *transform* your organization and empower your employees to do the same. To do so, an inclusive mind-set must replace uninformed assumptions about different groups of people. In the next chapter, I will discuss the most common uninformed assumptions around diversity and inclusion so that we can begin to explore their impact on workplace culture and practices.

The Language of Diversity

---

*The assumptions you hold about those different
from you, whether unconscious or not, are present in
all of your experiences and interactions.*

**Real diversity, equity, and inclusion requires a whole new
approach**, a broader and richer mind-set to see the value inherent
in normalizing the presence of all kinds of people within the corporate community—the same kinds of people who will consume your
goods and services.

The first step in broadening your perspective is understanding the language behind diversity and the commonplace acts that
prevent (i.e., lip service) or promote (i.e., beyond lip service) the
creation of an inclusive environment. Awareness has to come before
we can understand where we and others need to do better. Here is
what you need to know before we begin our deep self-exploration
to get to the root causes of resistance to diversity and inclusion.

DIVERSITY

To attain diversity means to develop a workforce with representatives from many different groups—for example, race, gender, age, sexual orientation, abilities, and cultural background.

LIP SERVICE: Hiring one or two people of color or according to other aspects of diversity and putting them on display as if "diversity" has been achieved.

BEYOND LIP SERVICE: Taking a critical look at business imperatives and hiring stellar diverse talent to meet business needs. These diverse hires are welcomed as critical for the business success of the organization based on their merit and unique contributions—for example, hiring qualified Hispanic-American advertising professionals to design a multimillion-dollar campaign for Product X aimed at communities of color.

INCLUSION

Inclusion means making it possible for individuals of different groups to succeed by creating a workplace that values who they are and what they offer, and provides opportunities for them to develop their full potential.

LIP SERVICE: An official "Everyone is welcomed here!" corporate declaration when, unofficially, everyone knows that the way to get ahead is to conform to the standards created by the dominant paradigm of corporate life. In other words, the company operates under a "get in where you fit in" or assimilation philosophy.

BEYOND LIP SERVICE: Having an established onboarding practice that connects new hires immediately with mentors, support and resources to allow for their successful integration into the corporate culture and to set them up for success. There are ongoing and routine check-ins so that leaders can take the pulse of the employees' experience throughout the first eighteen months. Finally, there are dedicated talent-management opportunities for diverse populations, including succession planning, with widely communicated goals and benchmarks.

PRIVILEGE

Privilege refers to rights, benefits, and advantages exclusively granted to particular groups of people. It is part of a much larger system that exists to protect the majority and its power. In the United States, privilege is granted to people who belong to one or more of the following social identity groups:

+ European-American people
+ Able-bodied people
+ Heterosexuals
+ Males
+ Christians
+ Middle- or owning-class people
+ Middle-aged people
+ English-speaking people

LIP SERVICE: When you are told that the company operates on a meritocracy and everyone has an equal chance to have their voice heard and get ahead. In reality, however, there are two sets of rules—one for the privileged class and one for everyone else. Everyone knows it, but it is taboo to call out or even talk about. A male senior executive can present his quarterly business report sprinkled with a few expletives, raising his voice or even hitting the table, and he is viewed as "passionate" and a "real go-getter." However, a woman exhibiting the same behavior is viewed as "overly emotional" and "too aggressive."

BEYOND LIP SERVICE: Only one set of rules is applied (with accountability) to ensure equity. This helps mitigate the effects of systemic bias and other forms of systemic oppression and inequity. It means that competency-based assessments are in place for all employees and that diverse voices are at the table for reviewing performance. Inequities are challenged and addressed with zero tolerance.

For a deeper exploration of the problem and power of privilege, please see chapter 3.

UNCONSCIOUS BIAS

Unconscious bias includes the prejudices and stereotypes for and against various characteristics formed without an individual's awareness. It is the filter we unknowingly place on ideas coming from diverse groups of people. Characteristics that frequently evoke bias include gender identity, race, ethnicity, age, sexual orientation, weight, and religion, among many others.

LIP SERVICE: When everyone in a company is made to attend an unconscious bias training workshop, and that's the end of the story. It does not lead to a decrease in employee discrimination.

BEYOND LIP SERVICE: While it is impossible to remove all bias from the workplace, moving beyond lip service requires doing the self-work necessary to acknowledge our biases and understand how they affect our decisions in business and beyond, and then using our privilege and influence for the betterment of our organization as a whole—including those employees whom we may have biases against. Practically, this requires a holistic approach to sustained behavioral change, including but not limited to: ongoing skill and knowledge development, using case studies with application exercises, coaching, and assessments for progress.

INTERSECTIONALITY

Twenty-eight years ago, Kimberlé Crenshaw coined the term *intersectionality* in a paper as a way to help explain the oppression of African-American women. Intersectionality is a two-part concept. First, it recognizes the complex experience of being a multifaceted person, an acknowledgment of the compounded identities within each person, such as being African-American and female and having a middle-class suburban upbringing. Second, it is the analysis of how different people with different identities interact with other people and systems.

LIP SERVICE: When companies commit to gender diversity and gender equality, but their impact is only realized by mostly white women. In truth, they are just replacing white male privilege with white female privilege.

BEYOND LIP SERVICE: Ensuring that all women of all origins and abilities and who represent all other aspects of diversity are included in their programs, initiatives, and goals. There is more than just one employee resource group and talent program for women to ensure segmentation across the various intersections of diversity and see that no group falls through the cracks.

MICROAGGRESSIONS

Microaggressions are subtle comments or actions that demonstrate bias against an individual from a marginalized group. Whether intentional or not, these instances, which often masquerade as good intentions or, worse, enlightenment, have the effect of nullifying a person's individuality and humanity as well as perpetuating inequality in and outside of the workplace.

Color blindness and *whitewashing* are examples of common microaggressions that deal with race.

☛ An increasingly popular way that some have discovered to circumvent the actual work involved in facing internalized prejudices and biased assumptions is to declare that they "don't see color"—or any other difference, for that matter.

What they're really doing is minimizing the experiences of others that differ from their own.

For example, Chadwick is a good African-American guy whom John, a white male, knows and likes. Chadwick is well aware that when John states he is "color-blind," he is indicating that he has no desire to learn about and understand Chadwick's different background, perspectives, and insights. Instead, John prefers to "whitewash" Chadwick's difference, effectively erasing Chadwick's uniqueness—one of the most valuable assets he brings to the table—along with it.

The very nature of a microaggression makes the person subjected to the behavior feel that the actions, words, and attitudes are too small to report without being perceived as being oversensitive or even petty. This dynamic allows the perpetrators to hide behind excuses like "Just joking" or "Lighten up," or claim ignorance about the impact of their words and actions. But microaggressions have the impact of water dripping on a rock—they eventually wear down even the strongest person if left unchecked.

LIP SERVICE: Below are microaggressions that people of diverse groups are often subjected to but that go under the radar of most companies' discrimination policies.

UNPACKING COMMON MICROAGGRESSIONS

Microaggression	Discriminatory message it implies
Saying "I don't see color."	A person of color's racial/ethnic experiences are unimportant.
Asking an Asian person to help with math or science projects.	All Asians are intelligent and good at math and science.
Using the pronoun "he" to refer to all people.	The male experience is universal, while the female experience is meaningless.
Assuming there are only two options for relationship status: married and single.	LGBTQIA partnerships do not matter.
Mistaking a female doctor for a nurse	Women only occupy nurturing, subsidiary roles.

Source: Adapted from Derald Wing Sue and David Sue's *Counseling the Culturally Diverse: Theory and Practice,* 5th Edition (John Wiley & Sons, 2008).

BEYOND LIP SERVICE: Creating a safe space for diverse groups to talk with others about the microaggressions and other bias-driven interactions they have faced in order to bring them—and their negative impact on diversity and inclusion—out into the open so they can be addressed head-on. In addition, leadership and HR must implement a policy for documenting microaggressions to determine trends versus an isolated offhand and irresponsible comment.

CODE-SWITCHING AND COVERING

Code-switching refers to alternating between multiple languages and behaviors based on circumstances and environment. In its mildest form, it is a way of assimilating in order to better connect with the people around you.

☛ Taken to the extreme, code-switching can morph into *covering*, which is the denial of certain core parts of yourself in order to be accepted.

Covering is an attempt to keep a stigmatized aspect of one's identity from playing a prominent role in one's interactions. The usual modus operandi across many companies is to apply an assimilation approach: you have to get in, blend in, and fit in. For many people of color, various gender identities, and different cultural backgrounds, their level of success is determined by their degree of assimilation with the common behaviors and practices of the organization. Covering is essentially a requirement.

Kenji Yoshino, the Chief Justice Earl Warren Professor of Constitutional Law at NYU, identified four categories under which covering tends to fall:

+ *Appearances:* Altering aspects of one's appearance, such as hairstyle or clothing, to fit into the dominant culture.

+ *Affiliation:* Attempting to shirk stereotypes frequently associated with one's identity by limiting or eliminating certain behaviors in public or at work.

+ *Advocacy:* Refraining from speaking up on behalf of one's identity group in order to prevent criticism or being singled out.

+ *Association:* Limiting interactions with other members of one's identity group to avoid being associated with them, as well as any corresponding stereotypes.[1]

Researchers surveyed employees across ten industries with the goal of measuring the frequency of covering for various identity groups. They found that 61 percent of respondents covered some aspect of their identity, including 45 percent of straight white men.[2] Moreover, the majority of respondents reported that covering was "somewhat detrimental" to "extremely detrimental" to their sense of self—almost everyone who covered also experienced a corresponding negative impact.

LIP SERVICE: Expecting that all men want to engage in "manly" conversations about sports, women, and cars. Furthermore, the more comfortable and adept you are in those topics, the easier it is for you to navigate the corporate ladder.

Another example is the inherent perception of whiteness as smart, professional, and valid whereas ethnicity in expression is considered less professional. This requires people of color to perform in ways that contradict the ill-informed perceptions of their race. They have to constantly think through their tone, word choice, posture, body language, and general demeanor in order to conform to a false standard. Trying to ensure that you don't say the "wrong" thing creates a constant state of anxiety.

BEYOND LIP SERVICE: Developing a bar for excellence in performance that is based on objective competencies instead of a flawed power dynamic that sets one race, language, or style as the norm and standard for everyone else to follow. It entails encouraging and supporting all employees in being authentic and bringing their unique contributions to the organization. Ultimately, it means that the core, common, and consistent expectations for excellence and professionalism are based on business needs and not interpersonal preferences.

NOW YOU KNOW

My goal in this chapter is to make you aware of any possible blind spots, particularly if you are part of the power construct. It is not to call you out or point fingers, but rather to help ensure that both the majority and minority members of society have a mutual understanding of what goes into creating an inclusive versus a discriminatory environment. Privilege is a tricky thing because you often don't know when it's working in your favor—or against someone else. In fact, privilege is such a thorny topic that I'm devoting the entire next chapter to discussing it—and explaining why this book is targeted to those who benefit the most from it.

CHAPTER 3

The Problem of Privilege: Does Diversity Mean I Lose Mine?

You can't give your privilege away, but you can use it for noble purposes.

You've most likely experienced the effects of privilege—whether or not you knew it *and* whether or not the effects were favorable (though the more beneficial they were, the less likely you were to notice them).

People with privilege are often oblivious to it. Rather than recognizing that having the many advantages granted to them is simply due to their privilege, they believe that the benefits they experience on a daily basis are due to their own efforts. Similarly, they often feel that those who do not have the same abundance of gifts go without for lack of trying.

Privilege—and institutional and systemic privilege in particular —generates a lot of controversy and debate, primarily because acknowledging privilege requires that members of the dominant group recognize that they did not earn many of the gifts they enjoy and that those gifts come at the expense of others. As Peggy McIntosh, former associate director of the Wellesley Centers for Women, so aptly wrote:

"I have come to see white privilege as an invisible package of unearned assets that I can count on cashing in each day, but about which I was 'meant' to remain oblivious. . . . White privilege is like an invisible weightless knapsack of special provisions, maps, passports, codebooks, visas, clothes, tools, and blank checks. Describing white privilege makes one newly accountable."[1]

In order to move toward a more inclusive society, the primary beneficiaries of privilege—namely European-American, heterosexual, Christian men—must recognize the advantages they are automatically granted. But the goal in addressing privilege is not to antagonize white men, but to involve them in the process and encourage their accountability, because we will only make progress if all of us—especially those in positions of power—are on board. While white men must recognize their privilege, the rest of us must recognize that for them, this new accountability will come with a sense of loss and discomfort:

"For white men, they have to give something up to get diversity, a cherished fact or assumption. One that isn't a fact," said Luke Visconti, founder and CEO of DiversityInc, at the 2018 DiversityInc Top 50 event, crediting the idea to John Campbell at Wells Fargo. He went on, "For me it was the assumption that this was a very fair country, that all you had to do was do your hardest and try your best, and you would be successful. What I've learned since then is that no matter how hard you try, you may be thwarted from being successful for reasons completely beyond your control: racism, sexism, ableism. Think about it. Religiousism. All of these things. Once, for you white men, you get over the disoriented process of being an old dog learning new tricks, I think you'll find it extremely rewarding and the best journey you've taken in your entire life."[2]

Acknowledging that we are part of an unfair system means giving up some of the blind spots that make institutional and societal structures palatable for many of those in the majority, and gaining some of the discomfort that comes with a new level of awareness. Doing so also allows for a visceral understanding of what minority colleagues have to deal with on a day-to-day basis.

A more diverse and inclusive workplace—and world—can be discomfiting to those in the majority in other ways. Many white men secretly fear that D&I means giving up their power to other groups. After all, if you were used to living in an environment that totally catered to your way of being where you had all the say, and someone told you that you had to give it up, your first reaction might be resistance, too.

Of course, no matter how understandable, this resistance needs to be dismantled. My approach is to get to the root causes of apathy and resistance to D&I via Inclusion Coaching and the COMMIT coaching model, which I explain in the next chapter. It uses empowering questions that engage individuals within the power structure in order to guide them on their personal journey toward embracing true diversity and inclusion.

While this empathetic approach may rub some diverse populations the wrong way at first, I believe that as a society we have to start where we are.

> ☞ These are the people who hold the power and the purse strings, and if we can't engage them on a deeper level, we will not see results. We need them to graciously, not begrudgingly, acknowledge and ultimately use their privilege to further the D&I cause.

And though the process may be unpleasant for all those involved at first, we can be allies, walking side by side on the journey toward inclusion.

In one of my coaching sessions, an executive-level sales leader shared that as a white man, he had been made aware of his privilege, but he was never told what to do about it. As a result, he was left feeling guilty about and disconnected from the ongoing diversity and inclusion conversations happening in his organization. Since he was a key decision-maker for organizational policies, this meant that those D&I conversations weren't having much of an impact on the company's practices.

Over time, our coaching sessions helped him reframe his privilege and become aware of the many everyday benefits he is afforded based solely on the fact that he is a member of the majority across multiple categories: a heterosexual, Christian, European-American man in a position of power. My client found one of the reflection questions to be especially empowering, facilitating a transformational shift for him:

◆   *How can you use your privilege to honor your values?*

Through the subsequent exploration and self-reflection he engaged in to answer this question, he discovered that he could use his power and privilege to actively participate in and further the diversity and inclusion work in his organization, rather than feeling ostracized by it.

A colleague of mine shared his story of waking up to his white male privilege—and what he chose to do next.

> *At fifty years of age, finally, I woke up to my White Male Privilege. And I'm glad to tell you—especially if you're white or male or both, like me—waking up has been a growth experience. Rather than causing me to feel guilty or defensive—though I sometimes slip into that space, I admit— I'm happy to share that, for the most part, waking up to my White Male Privilege makes me feel responsible, engaged, and sometimes hopeful.*
>
> *Now, to be honest, I'll tell you that I also feel a bit disappointed in myself. All my life I told myself I was one of "the good guys." I was born and raised in Massachusetts in a working-class family. I've adhered all my life to progressive values. I came out as gay in my early twenties. I attended a top-notch university and traveled the world extensively working for economic and social development. I've volunteered for causes like cancer research, LGBT youth suicide prevention, and social services for newly arrived immigrants.*
>
> *The "bad people" propagate racism and male chauvinism. I've always distinguished myself from "those people" with "not me" rationalizations: not me, my family worked hard just to*

make a modest living. Not me, I'm a lifelong progressive. Not me, I'm gay—one of the oppressed. Not me, I've worked to help the less fortunate. Not me, I'm a deeply empathetic person—ask anyone!

For decades, I sang myself a "not me" lullaby to maintain my comfortable slumber of denial until a confluence of events created enough noise to jar me awake. In the world around me, I was stirred by displays of newly emboldened white supremacy on the one hand and the shocking truths exposed by the #MeToo movement on the other hand. In my professional experiences, I was prodded by a sudden and persistent pattern of (mostly young) voices raised in the workplace challenging deeply ingrained and dangerously subtle patterns of discrimination.

My awakening began gradually until one day the shades were thrown open. I was conducting a leadership development workshop for a client. My material calls out different styles of leadership, one of which I call the "Trustworthy Citizen." The idea is to suggest that sometimes being a leader is simply about modeling behaviors of a cooperative member of the workplace community. After I presented the concept, one member of the group spoke up, pointing out that the word "citizen" aligned with white supremacist rhetoric and that she and others in the room were uncomfortable with my language. I could feel the tips of my ears burning as I attempted a reassuring reply.

"Thank you for sharing your view. That's important to hear. But let's not get hung up on my word choices; let's focus on the idea I'm trying to convey. I'm not here as a diversity expert, I'm just here to talk about leadership skills."

My assurances did not have the effect I hoped for, and for a few minutes I presided over what was for me an extremely awkward and uncomfortable conversation, ending with my retreating to this: "I feel uncomfortable facilitating this conversation, especially as a middle-aged white guy."

That was it. That was the moment I fully woke up, albeit in a daze. I was fully exposed to the light of my privileged effort to escape the moment because it was uncomfortable.

Things had turned awkward for me, and so in my position of power as the outside expert and a middle-aged white male, I was shutting it down. When I heard the suggestion that my leadership material could somehow be associated with white supremacy, I freaked out. I was panicked, guilt-ridden, and defiant all at once.

"No, not me," said my inside voice, "I'm a good guy."

What made this moment unique was that I saw all of this playing out in my mind. I recognized that even while I intended to appear humble and understanding by admitting that I was ill-equipped to handle this situation, I was exercising my privilege to escape it. And although I was able to see this, I wasn't able to stop myself from giving an inadequate answer in the moment. But once we wrapped up the session, I was able to say to myself, "Now that you can see, you need to learn to speak. Next time, you need to have a better response."

Waking up is only the first step. The ability to see my White Male Privilege is the beginning of a longer process. Since that moment of new clarity, I've taken responsibility for learning some new language. I've begun searching for resources to educate myself. I've shared my waking-up story in videos posted on LinkedIn. I've begun to organize a small experimental group of other white male professionals who share an interest in waking up and learning how to engage productively to address racism and male chauvinism in their community and workplace.

White Male Privilege is not a mark of shame. White Male Privilege is a social reality that's been passed down to us and that we perpetuate through complacent slumber. When we first wake up to it, we might feel defensive or guilty. We're also human beings, and so those feelings are understandable, but defensiveness and guilt don't serve us if we then wish to contribute to positive change.

I am awake and I am seeking to learn what I can do with that clarity. I'm ready to find ways to use owning the fact of my White Male Privilege as a tool for doing even more good.

PRIVILEGE AS A PLATFORM

Regardless of your identity, you have the power, privilege, and opportunity to make a difference that benefits everyone. Rather than denying it or avoiding the inclusion conversation, participate; it's vital to our collective success.

I encourage those with privilege—white men, in particular—to stretch toward change with humility and curiosity about what is possible when we commit to moving forward in unity toward a culture of inclusion. I also encourage women, people of color, members of the LGBTQIA community, and individuals from other demographics to become curious about what white men need relative to D&I.

◆ *Do they have a sense of belonging in diversity work, or are they expected to passively support from the fringe?*

◊ *Are white men diverse?*

◊ *How does D&I affect white men?*

◊ *What is their inclusion story?*

◊ *What are the issues that lie deep beneath the surface for white men?*

For those of you reading this who are not white males: hear me out.

☛ Diversity and inclusion goes all ways. It cannot be about condemning white men as the oppressor or throwing stones.

Yes, we all need to acknowledge the reality that European-American males in America—and many other places around the world—have privilege that others don't. We must also accept that that privilege provides a platform, a platform we can use to raise our D&I standards.

Asking *How can privilege be used in a way that moves us forward together?* can be a powerful starting point for progress and make the conversation an easier one for everyone.

Take Brad, for example. Brad is a six-foot-three, straight white guy; a former linebacker; and a VP of operations at a large banking institution. He was visibly nervous as he opened Chandler Bank's regional board meeting, addressing his peers and several national leaders.

He cleared his throat and said in a resolute tone, "Good morning, we have some work to do relative to attracting and retaining diverse talent and building an inclusive culture here at Chandler Bank—and I believe that we, as white men, can lead the way by using our privilege to benefit everyone."

There was a long, awkward silence as the group took in what Brad had just said. Finally, his colleague Rich spoke up. "I'm open to exploring ways to improve our culture, but don't you think we are setting ourselves up for some real criticism if we take the lead on this? I mean, look around the room. We're not exactly the face of diversity."

"That's exactly why we need to support and address the issues surrounding inclusion, diversity, equality, and gender in the workplace," Brad replied. "This room is full of decision-makers, and we're the ones who need to take action. We can use our influence to create safe spaces for our employees to openly discuss the barriers and opportunities here at Chandler. We can start by increasing the number of women in senior-level positions and addressing the fact that we're hemorrhaging African-American employees."

There was a full range of responses as members began to chime in around the table. Some of the leaders were vehemently opposed to the idea, while others were curious about where this could take the organization.

Brad offered to lead by sharing his D&I journey and subsequently opened a company-wide dialogue. He spoke about his experience coming to grips with his privilege and how he wanted to use it for noble purposes now. The group aligned around the concept and agreed to publish Brad's story on the internal company blog as a first step in building awareness.

Unsurprisingly, the employees of Chandler Bank—who were far more diverse than its leadership—were ready and willing to begin the D&I conversation: Brad's blog post received a record number of positive responses.

HELPING WHITE MEN UNPACK THEIR TRUTH

While Brad serves as a fantastic example of using one's privilege for progress, people often need help recognizing not only their privilege, but also how to use it for good. As coaches and managers, we can help white men unpack their truth regarding privilege in the workplace and recognize the unfair advantages that influence their decisions, ranging from hiring and promotions to professional development and compensation. Doing so effectively requires that we create a safe space where white men and other privileged groups can go deep within themselves to discover and share their truth about their privilege and bias—openly and candidly—without guilt or judgment. Understandably, going deep to discover and reveal truths about a sensitive topic like privilege may be uncomfortable for many leaders, but it is necessary for progress.

As a professional coach, I'm very keen to maintain compassion while allowing for those I coach to embrace the discomfort that is often associated with looking in all of their mirrors—not just the ones that capture their best side. It has been quite remarkable to work with leaders who are confronting powerful questions like the ones below for the first time:

- ◆ *What is your relationship with privilege? What do you want it to be?*

- ◆ *What role has privilege played in your career?*

- ◆ *How has privilege affected the non-majority employees in your organization?*

- ◆ *How does bias show up in your interactions with employees unlike yourself?*

☛ It can be an exhilarating and exhausting experience for leaders to face parts of themselves that they might not have been aware of previously.

That said, it is important that we let employees fully express all that they feel as they interrogate their perspective, decisions, and actions in and out of the workplace. Interjecting too much has the potential to dilute their experience.

If it gets ugly, let them deal with the ugly. I've witnessed transformational change in clients on the other side of ugly; it often required dark or upsetting revelations along the way. These startling revelations lie tucked away in clients' blind spots, even when they are glaringly obvious to others.

THE POWER OF PRIVILEGE

At the office, many of us wave away the discomfort of exclusion with a multitude of excuses, some more plausible than others. We blame the homogeneous character of our organizations on the lack of "qualified" diverse candidates to explain our inability to attract and retain diverse talent; or we categorize sexist, racist, or homophobic jokes and comments as harmless "guy talk." We let others' behavior slide even when we know in our hearts that it is hurtful, inappropriate, or even damaging to an organization's progress.

One of the reasons for inaction on diversity and inclusion is that people don't want to be called out or dropped from the favor and privilege of the dominant culture. This makes sense; of course, no one *wants* to be excluded. Reflecting on Brad's experience earlier in the chapter, it took a lot of courage for him to take a stand for D&I, especially among a very homogeneous group of peers. He knew that he could be putting himself at odds with the rest of the team by speaking up—but he decided to honor his values, push past his fear, and act for the betterment of the organization.

When we speak, we want people to listen. When we make contributions at work, we want recognition for those contributions. Just as white men don't want to have their career progress judged as being a product of privilege and unfair advantages, people of color do not want to be judged as being tokens to meet a representation quota. If we are part of a team, we all want to be acknowledged as qualified, valuable contributors—a courtesy that everyone deserves. Those who are not part of the majority are not asking for privilege or special handling, just fair and equal treatment—the same kind we all want.

☛ It is imperative that we look within and realize that what we hold most dear is our values, and the only way to preserve those values is to ensure that we are not hindering anyone else's access to fair and equal treatment.

For us to do so, inclusion must be a part of every facet of our lives, from dining room table discussions all the way to the boardroom.

Privilege is part of a much larger system that exists to protect the majority and its power, and the unconscious biases support that system. That said, the goal of Inclusion Coaching is not to remove privilege and bias from the workplace (which is impossible anyway). Rather, it is to meet people where they are so that they can do the self-work necessary to acknowledge their truth, understand how it affects their decisions in business and beyond, and use their privilege for the betterment of the organization as a whole—including those employees who are not afforded the same opportunities.

Regardless of which segment of society we are a part of—whether it's the majority or a minority, male or female, straight or gay, able-bodied or disabled—we must remember that we all want the same things from life and understand that in order to ensure that others have them as well, we can't accept excuses from anyone—even ourselves. This is why I believe that coaching—and the accountability it brings—is a powerful and effective way to move D&I forward.

CHAPTER 4

Coaching + D&I = Δ Behavior

Coaching unleashes the radical truth and transformative power that lies dormant within each of us.

The International Coach Federation defines coaching as "partnering with clients in a thought-provoking and creative process that inspires them to maximize their personal and professional potential." I offer inclusion as the next platform of coaching, a niche area of expertise alongside performance, executive, and relationship coaching that addresses the growing need to challenge bias and build authentic cultures where everyone can feel a sense of belonging in our organizations and in our lives.

I believe that Inclusion Coaching is the way to overcome D&I resistance because it starts engaging individuals where they are, without judgment. For example, instead of being told at a D&I training session that you need to be "more inclusive," to have more diverse hires, and to make sure that everyone can recite your D&I policy, you can have an Inclusion Coach work with you from the inside out to support you in facing your own biases and resistance in order to break it down yourself and move toward a more inclusive mind-set and more inclusive actions.

Magdalena Mook, CEO and executive director of the International Coach Federation, says, "Coaches empower their clients to become the expert of their own lives and experiences. This personal accountability is critical in promoting a diverse and inclusive workplace where everyone, from entry-level employees to executive leadership, can 'walk the talk.'"[1]

My primary goal as an Inclusion Coach is to ensure that the needs of others are being met and that they can fulfill their potential. Thus, each Inclusion Coaching journey begins with organizations digging deep to answer a fundamental question: "In what are you asking people to be included?"

From there, I encourage individuals to go deep within themselves to discover their own power, resourcefulness, and inherent wisdom. I provoke these realizations by asking a series of empowering questions, encouraging clients to be curious about the individuals with whom they're working and to be curious about themselves.

Let's go back to Vanessa from chapter 1 who felt sorely excluded and dismissed as an African-American woman working in the predominantly white-male environment at Setco. What if Setco had decided to take its commitment to increasing diversity to the next level instead of just filling slots on its teams with diverse candidates? What if they had hired a coach who was experienced in cultivating diversity, equity, and inclusion among organizations and employees, or used some of the Inclusion Coaching strategies we'll discuss here to support both the company's leadership team and new hires? Rather than losing high-potential players like Vanessa to more inclusive companies ready and willing to capitalize on their talents, Setco could have worked to become more inclusive itself, prepared both parties to communicate effectively, and reaped the many rewards of an open and inclusive environment.

In the following passage, one of my colleagues offers an inside look at her experience with Inclusion Coaching.

The complexities of many situations we face challenge us to question and redefine beliefs we may have previously had that were much simpler. Balancing the desire to take action and speak up for yourself or others with the need to maintain professionalism and anonymity can feel like entering a gray area at times.

There is a difference between knowing something intellectually and understanding it at a visceral level, beyond our own ego or judgment. I've found that at the root of all of the difficult situations I've faced is this: Everything you wish to see or experience starts with you. We may not be able to choose all of the situations we find ourselves in, but we can always choose to focus internally and maintain the power to assess with true clarity.

One of the most important things I have and continue to take away from Inclusion Coaching is the incredible power and consequence speaking your truth has on one of the most invaluable assets you possess: your self-respect. Finding a way to make sure this is honored in a way that feels empowering is one of the most important lessons I continue to learn, in every aspect of my life.

This is exactly what Inclusion Coaching aims to do: help people embrace their truths and build a path forward by exploring unconscious bias, conscious choice, and courageous action.

UNCONSCIOUS BIAS, CONSCIOUS CHOICE, AND COURAGEOUS ACTION

◆ *How do we approach a situation where a client has been subjected to racist, sexist, or exclusionary behavior in the workplace?*

◆ *How do we address issues such as multicultural conflict and microaggressions? How do we work with leaders who are struggling with their privilege?*

◆ *How do we maximize company potential with an increasingly diverse employee population?*

No organization is immune to the complex issues that can arise when people of different backgrounds and experiences work together. Inclusion Coaching helps to resolve these issues by focusing on three core principles:

+ *Unconscious bias:* What are my thoughts and beliefs that unwittingly marginalize or discriminate against diverse groups?

+ *Conscious choice:* What choices am I making day in and day out toward creating and upholding a welcoming and inclusive workplace culture?

+ *Courageous action:* How can I respectfully challenge and call out biases, rather than relying on higher-ups or HR representatives to handle these situations?

THREE CORE PRINCIPLES OF INCLUSION COACHING

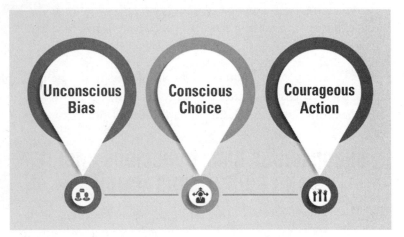

UNCONSCIOUS BIAS

Many organizations provide unconscious bias training, but few understand how to take unconscious bias training out of the classroom and make it both actionable and sustainable. Some lose confidence in the value of unconscious bias training when expected outcomes don't materialize, but without a series of steps to take after the training ends, it's hard—if not impossible—to make that valuable information actionable.

Relying solely on training is a recipe for failure; we must also coach people to help them understand what to do with their newly discovered biases. Numerous clients of mine have said something to the effect of, "I learned that I have bias at a recent training, but I am not sure where to go from here." Identifying next steps is a crucial piece of the puzzle.

Instead of people leaving a workshop with the nebulous goal of increasing diversity and inclusion, Inclusion Coaching can support them in continuing to identify their biases in their daily lives and deciding what they can commit to do differently based on that knowledge. In addition, it offers them ongoing opportunities to reflect and be accountable.

Take the April 2018 incident that occurred at a Philadelphia Starbucks, in which two black men were arrested after asking to use the restroom. They were told that the store's restrooms were only for customers, and when they remained at the location to wait for an acquaintance without purchasing anything—a common practice at virtually every Starbucks—the store's manager called the police. The episode was labeled as one of implicit or unconscious bias by Philadelphia's police commissioner, the city's mayor, the National Association for the Advancement of Colored People (NAACP), and patrons who witnessed the men being removed from the premises.[2]

The NAACP also weighed in on the Starbucks manager's decision to call the police and the subsequent arrests. NAACP CEO Derrick Johnson stated, "The Starbucks situation provides dangerous insight regarding the failure of our nation to take implicit bias seriously. . . . We refuse to believe that our unconscious bias—the racism we are unaware of—can and does make its way into our actions and policies."[3]

To address the incident and corresponding questions about implicit bias, Starbucks closed more than eight thousand U.S. stores for a racial bias training on May 29, 2018.

"While this is not limited to Starbucks, we're committed to being part of the solution. Closing our stores for racial bias training is just one step in a journey that requires dedication from every level of our company and partnerships in local communities,"[4] said Starbucks CEO Kevin Johnson.

What Starbucks could have done was take its unconscious bias training further, helping to integrate the information learned during training into participants' consciousness for the long term. Inclusion Coaching could have supported employees in unpacking and digesting their personal experiences in the training and in their lives by encouraging them to go deep within themselves and identify the lens through which they saw the world. It is this level of introspection that helps us understand how our biases affect our perspectives in virtually every situation. It also provides insight into the limits of our own thinking, bringing to light the unconscious considerations that do not disappear when we are building or leading our teams.

The time is over for a "one and done" approach to D&I engagement. That is just lip service. To go beyond lip service, we must engage multiple resources and modalities for training, coaching, practice, and assessment. Accountability must also be addressed at the strategic level, including a dedicated learning continuum focused on how to make the training actionable and sustainable and how to foster long-term behavioral change. It is only when we are armed with the knowledge and strategies to face our unconscious biases that we can move past the guilt of our biases and consciously choose new ways to show up inside and outside of work.

CONSCIOUS CHOICE

Rather than focusing on removing our biases entirely—an impossible feat—we must shift our focus toward making conscious choices to confront and override those biases. This is where the real work happens.

Understanding our individual positions and progress when it comes to inclusion requires that we have a conversation with ourselves.

◆ *What choices are you making day in and day out relative to diversity and inclusion?*

◆ *How do you engage in or avoid issues that arise from differing perspectives in the workplace?*

◆ *How does inclusivity honor your values?*

☞ Only when we choose to be brutally honest with the person in the mirror can we begin to meaningfully consider the experience of others, especially those different from us.

Coaches can help build inclusion intelligence and maturity, moving beyond that one-time workshop or the pages in a book to help determine the areas that could benefit from self-work—whether on an individual, team, or organizational level—and dictate the steps necessary to start building a culture of inclusion.

☞ Increasing this awareness through coaching expands the capacity of an individual or an organization to embrace and explore possibilities and new ways of being.

Ultimately, heightened awareness aids us in making value-based decisions and in taking into account the meaning and impact of our choices. It allows us to be intentional—and hold ourselves accountable—for the day-to-day choices we make regarding inclusion.

COURAGEOUS ACTION

Maya Angelou once said, "Courage is the most important of all the virtues, because without courage you can't practice any other virtue consistently. You can practice any virtue erratically, but nothing consistently without courage."[5]

Courageous action requires challenging the status quo, and often our own preconceived notions and implicit biases, in order to create meaningful change in ourselves and in our environment. It involves respectfully calling out biases rather than relying on executive leaders or HR representatives to handle these situations. After all, bias—implicit or not—and exclusion can manifest at any level of an organization, from individuals in entry-level positions to the C-suite, and even in HR policies and the corporate culture itself. Cultivating a culture of diversity and inclusion is the responsibility of each member of an organization.

By acting courageously, you help operationalize inclusion, just like the students in this next example, shared by S. Barton Cutter, an accessibility consultant for the Coaches Training Institute (CTI):

"A student requested a sign-language interpreter. The cohort chose, collectively, to include the interpreter more fully in the group dynamic. This led to a whole new design within the classroom, where all students' learning was reinforced through watching the interpreter's physical expression. . . .

"Here, accommodations for professionals with unique and different abilities become less about *what they need* and more about *how their perspective uniquely informs and enhances the work process* [emphasis added]."[6]

Cutter discussed the impact of the group's courageous action in embracing the way in which their hearing-impaired colleague experienced the world, and how what is often seen as a limitation actually brought new value and awareness to the classroom experience.

COMMIT: THE "HOW" OF INCLUSION

Several years ago, leaders at an investment firm I'll call Smith & Ritter decided to take a concrete step toward fostering a corporate culture of diversity and inclusion, so they appointed a midlevel, well-liked manager to head up their newly launched D&I program.

Malcolm Wexler had been with the company for nearly a decade, knew his way around, and, because of his excellent people skills, could marshal support for the launch of an umbrella-like employee resource group (ERG) to encourage the growth of diverse employee affinity groups. By year two, Wexler's efforts had led to the creation of a dozen different groups that gathered together employees who were Hispanic, single moms, millennials, African-Americans, female executives, members of the LGBTQIA community, veterans, differently abled, and several other identities as well. All these affinity groups held social events designed to enhance their awareness and feeling of solidarity with one another. Through them, friendships and support networks formed, and the members of each group felt less excluded at work. Those were the good outcomes.

The not-so-good outcome was that event attendance dropped markedly after two years, with only a faithful few continuing to show up. It had become quite clear that what needed to change at Smith & Ritter hadn't been altered even slightly. The firm's systemic bias, which affected everyone not part of the majority, was still actively in place. Old-school company policies that did not account for diverse lifestyles and needs were as inflexibly applied as ever, and outdated hiring and promotion practices were perpetuated when career-development opportunities were covertly denied to those who weren't members of the preferred majority. As a result, employees continued to feel a need to hide parts of their core identity at work, which had the effect of depressing their full engagement on the job.

Wexler was deeply disappointed that there had been so little progress—especially given the initial enthusiasm and loyal partici- pation by so many. He felt this even more keenly on the day he met with the small group of leaders who'd originally championed his

D&I role at the company. Nothing else could be done, they told him. After all, everyone had tried their best, hadn't they?

Wexler was taken aback by their willingness to scrap the whole initiative, but he tried to remain calm while pointing out that real change would necessitate the collaboration of human resources and the sponsorship of diverse employees by top-level executives in order to alter the way that current employee practices had long been configured.

The leaders were clearly nonplussed by this idea. Changing the way employees were handled would require active involvement by members of the C-suite. But diversity and inclusion, they told Wexler, were not part of their overriding concerns; they were naturally more concerned about profitability and stockholders.

Wexler felt as if he were bailing water from a sinking boat with his bare hands as he mustered all his people skills in an effort to mollify these leaders. After conceding the reasonableness of their perspective, he went on to say that more could and *should* be done in the areas of diversity and inclusion. Smith & Ritter simply could not afford to be left behind in this critical area. Visibly irritated, several leaders tried to cover up their annoyance by laughing halfheartedly as they told Wexler he was "one persistent guy." They'd get back to him, they said, in a few weeks. Five weeks later, he was still waiting.

What happened with Malcolm Wexler's D&I program is far from unusual. Lip service leaders often focus on the appearance of change but don't know how to make inclusion an embedded reality.

Having repeatedly witnessed stalled-out inclusion scenarios like this one in my work and volunteerism as a diversity and inclusion advocate over the past three decades, and having mentored and coached leaders facing these challenges, I developed a coaching model to provide a framework for the "how" of inclusion—one that could help individuals and companies not only identify a better way but also act on it. Inclusion Coaching is the method; COMMIT is the model:

COMMIT: A SIMPLE, MEASURABLE, AND ACTIONABLE MODEL

The COMMIT coaching model brings structure to the Inclusion Coaching process. I designed it quite deliberately as a pragmatic way to move beyond the preliminary cultivation of awareness about the need for diversity and inclusion—the point at which so many initiatives come to a standstill. COMMIT leaps over that hurdle by offering a model and framework with clear guidelines for building a mind-set and environment where inclusion can thrive. Furthermore, it can be used

+ on yourself (self-coaching),
+ on others (manager/leader as coach for employees), and
+ as the foundation for broader D&I initiatives within your organization (training seminars, workshops, one-on-one sessions, ERGs etc.).

The methodology of COMMIT is embedded in its name, with each letter standing for one step in its six-step process:[7]

Commit to Courageous Action

Open Your Eyes and Ears

Move beyond Lip Service

Make Room for Controversy and Conflict

Invite New Perspectives

Tell the Truth Even When It Hurts

THE COMMIT MODEL

COMMIT COACHING QUESTIONS

Commit to Courageous Action
What is the contribution/difference you want to make?
What are you committed to?
What does success look like and how will you measure it?
How can you create a culture of inclusion?
What will you do? By when?

Open Your Eyes and Ears
What do you see?
What are you overlooking?
What can you stop tolerating?
What is it like to be you?
Who are you?

Move beyond Lip Service
What do you have that you are not using?
How can you take yourself to the edge and beyond?
What do you choose to take responsibility for, relative to inclusion?
If you were to raise the bar, what would it look like?
What would be possible if you did not censor yourself?

Make Room for Controversy and Conflict
What would the best version of you choose to do next?
What scares you about diversity and inclusion?
What can you say no to?
What's stopping you?
What would it cost you if things remained the same as they are?

Invite New Perspectives
Who are you becoming?
What is emerging?
What's possible?
What are your choices?
What will you do to stay aware of others' perspectives?

Tell the Truth Even When It Hurts
What do you care about in this situation?
When you talk to yourself about yourself, what do you say?
What truth would you like to share?
How does inclusivity honor your values?
What story do you tell yourself about people whose culture differs from yours?

☛ COMMIT guides coaches in asking individuals empowering questions that tap into their truths and ignite their curiosity about themselves and those who are different from them.

It abandons the "stairway" approach of most models and embraces a more fluid method so that individuals, teams, and organizations can opt in at a place that fits their unique inclusion journey. You can start with Tell the Truth Even When It Hurts, Commit to Courageous Action, or anywhere in between. What is important is that you start where you are.[8]

Not that that makes the whole process easy . . .

As much as we may like the idea of forward momentum and transformative change, in reality, most of us prefer the familiarity of our comfort zone—that's one hurdle. Then there's the incontrovertible fact that dominant cultures around the world have been dominant and in control for several hundred years, so they feel inherently more "normal" than anything else does, at least for many of the generations around today.

This is why I designed the COMMIT coaching framework to help individuals go deep within to face fears and deal with radical truths. It is how we begin to examine some of the challenges and opportunities that lie ahead, starting with Commit to Courageous Action.

CHAPTER 5

Commit to Courageous Action

Uncomfortable adjustments are needed to create workplaces that work for all instead of a select few.

- ◆ *What does it mean to be an inclusive leader?*
- ◆ *What is the difference you want to make?*
- ◆ *What are you committed to doing?*

When it comes to diversity and inclusion, we as a society have already taken *some* action and we've seen *some* incremental progress that should be celebrated. But now, we are at a critical juncture between good intentions and a still-less-than-ideal reality. It's time to go beyond presenting the business case, building awareness, and training in unconscious bias. It's time to go courageously into new territory: deep into the root causes of D&I resistance that are preventing real inclusion (not just lip service) from taking seed in the workplace.

So what does courageous action look like?

+ Challenging the status quo
+ Being open about where you are
+ Defining inclusive behaviors
+ Incentivizing and tracking inclusiveness

CHALLENGING THE STATUS QUO

It's one thing to verbalize your expectations for your organization to be inclusive; it's another to take the measures to ensure that inclusiveness is embedded in its DNA. Doing so often challenges the status quo—a necessary step to achieve meaningful change.

Take for example the extensive research that shows that increased female representation on boards is correlated with improved corporate performance.[1] Why is it that so many companies that know what they need to do to get better results still don't have women on their boards? Why as a society do we continue to have such a marked deficit in gender diversity at the top levels? I believe it's because the traditional "status quo" approaches to candidate selection perpetuate a cycle of going back to the same homogeneous talent pool that does not include women. And let's face it—the "pool" is not the problem. The real problem is a lack of intentionality, strategy, and execution.

☛ To effectively challenge the status quo, we must be willing to do things that have never been done before.

In this case, it would mean redefining selection criteria to not rely so heavily on previous executive and board experience because we know that executive and board positions have historically been held by European-American men. A more creative and courageous approach would be to focus on transferable skills, gaps based on the current board composition, and anticipated business needs in order to yield a broader pool of candidates—and ultimately a better board.

There have been a number of approaches to challenging the status quo and increasing female representation on corporate boards. Some are even contradictory—such as legislative mandates for specific percentages of gender diversity (as in California)[2] and the 30% Club, a collaborative campaign that doesn't believe in mandatory quotas. As their mission statement says, "The 30% Club aims to develop a diverse pool of talent for all businesses through the efforts of its Chair and CEO members who are committed to better gender balance at all levels of their organisations. Business leadership is key to our mission, taking the issue beyond a specialist diversity effort and into mainstream talent management."[3]

These two approaches shed light on the complexity associated with challenging the status quo. Which one is the correct approach? Truthfully, we don't know yet—and until we see meaningful change, we will have to embrace the complexity and uncertainty associated with doing things differently. Diversity and inclusion work is complicated, but we can't allow that to become an excuse for accepting the status quo and doing nothing.

Although it's been said previously, it bears repeating here: we should be challenging the status quo from one end of the organization to the other, from the ground floor through the C-suite to the board—bottom-up and top-down, working together to establish lasting change.

BEING OPEN ABOUT WHERE YOU ARE

You may fear the threat of harsh criticism for acknowledging your organization's lack of diversity, but in our current environment, you might just be met with an overwhelmingly positive response. Why? Because acknowledging where you are—along with the concrete steps you are taking for improvement—is a first real step to going beyond D&I lip service.

Committing to sharing current demographics and D&I goals with employees at every level—and even with stakeholders outside the organization—can be an incredibly effective motivational tool. Not only does it force a company to evaluate its present standing, but it requires leadership to articulate goals and note benchmarks along the way. What is more, a willingness to recognize a lack of diversity and make real strides to improve it models commitment and accountability that stakeholders and consumers alike can appreciate.

If your current level of diversity and inclusion is not where you would like it to be, courageously own where you are and move forward. Doing so requires a deeper level of vulnerability and transparency, both necessary tools to achieve meaningful change. Take Google, for example: They hit some very visible bumps along their path to inclusion but have nevertheless committed to being open in their process. They instituted an actionable, four-pronged approach that included work inside and outside their offices and made their efforts readily available on their website.[4] Below is their open acknowledgment of where they are:

> Google should be a place where people from different backgrounds and experiences come to do their best work—a place where every Googler feels they belong. The truth is that we're not there yet. We know diversity and inclusion are values critical to our success and future innovation. We also know challenging bias—inside and outside our walls—is the right thing to do. That's why we continue to support efforts that fuel our commitments to progress. These commitments require us to look at bias through a wider lens: at Google, in the industry, and in society. And while progress will take time, our actions today will determine who we are in the future.

The fact that an organization has a lot of work to do on diversity and inclusion shouldn't be an incriminating secret if the organization is willing to work on it. Making your D&I metrics public and publicly outlining your plans to improve demonstrates the seriousness with which your company is approaching the task at hand and serves as a valuable signal to diverse talent that your office is a place they may feel comfortable.

DEFINING INCLUSIVE BEHAVIORS

If you were to ask ten people to define inclusion, you would likely get ten definitions. That makes getting to the next level—defining and incentivizing inclusive behaviors—difficult. How can we teach leaders how to do something well if we don't necessarily agree on what they should be doing in the first place?

Here's a very practical example: If I were to tell you that inclusive leaders "respect the opinions of others," that would be a good insight. But you might reply that respecting the opinions of others is an important thing for *anyone* to do or wonder aloud about how to make that respect apparent in a business meeting. Now, if I tell you instead that inclusive leaders "proactively seek out others different from themselves, learn about their perspectives, and then work with them to create meaningful solutions," you would have a much better idea of how you as a leader can show your diverse team members that you care about their ideas—as well as help your organization benefit from their insights.

This reality drives home the importance of establishing the qualities of an inclusive leader and pinpointing the behaviors that can make a real difference in fostering a culture of inclusion. It can feel a little risky to dive into D&I discussions without fully knowing what you're walking into—it's uncharted territory for the majority of us—but doing so will demonstrate your personal commitment to inclusivity and enhance your employees' experience. It is most effective to approach these discussions around what it means to be inclusive and what inclusive behaviors look like from a place of curiosity. Coaching leaders through a series of empowering questions about D&I can help them devise a clear and unified approach to establishing a culture of inclusion. Go deep to explore these subjects:

+ The purpose of diversity and inclusion at your organization
+ The strategies necessary to fulfill that purpose
+ The capacity of the organization to achieve its goals
+ How management systems can support that strategy to involve everyone, at all levels in the conversation

☛ True alignment requires a collaborative rather than a top-down approach.

Those involved must be able to weigh in, share concerns, and bring their authentic selves to the table without fear of judgment. Encouraging your leaders to become curious about what they may be hearing instead of automatically trying to shut it down will also help open the door for these new and courageous conversations around the "how" of change. Cultivating an environment in which everyone feels supported in taking risks and is comfortable with being uncomfortable will pave the way for a strategy that resonates with all members of the team and facilitate buy-in on a deeper level. It will urge them to act, not just comply.

INCENTIVIZING AND MEASURING INCLUSIVENESS

Of course, not every employee is going to be motivated to get on the D&I train, especially those who see diversity and inclusion as encroaching on the space that has traditionally been carved out just for them. This is why leadership must convey that D&I is a business imperative rather than a mere recommendation.

Approaches to incentivizing D&I span the goal-setting spectrum. Some organizations take the easy route, setting vague targets such as "Increase diversity in senior leadership," while others shoot for the stars with goals such as "Fifty percent gender parity in two years." At first glance, it may seem that the latter leans more toward courageous action, but not necessarily. The reality is that without appropriate levels of assessment, strategy, and execution, both of these goals can amount to empty promises.

I encourage you, as an executive leader in your organization, to treat D&I goals with the same level of gravity and accountability as sales goals. I spent more than a decade as a sales leader for large multinational organizations, and neither I nor my team ever had the option of simply "trying" to promote our products. We either hit our sales goals or we didn't. And we were either rewarded or penalized accordingly.

While measuring "inclusiveness" requires more creativity than analyzing D&I indicators that are strictly quantitative, like employee demographics, it is just as crucial, if not more so. For some leaders, this can become another hurdle to achieving desired outcomes: if the method of measurement is different from the metrics they are used to, it may seem more justifiable to instead put the same energy and funding into sales or marketing, where results appear more concrete. But as we know, inclusion can have an equally significant impact on productivity and profit.

☛ Building these metrics with the business side of the organization in mind can help ensure that all stakeholders understand the value of your inclusion strategy.

This is a great place to engage your business leaders with empowering questions like "How can D&I serve as an enabler to your business growth?"

One example is establishing goals for developing a sustainable pipeline of diverse talent. When a strong pipeline is developed and maintained, the issue with ensuring that one or two diverse candidates are included in interview slates is diminished. Another example is shifting the focus to term limits on corporate boards to help drive gender parity.

Additional metrics to gauge inclusiveness often take more qualitative forms, such as employee-engagement surveys, 360 evaluations, and focus groups. Organizations can also take a high-level view of their progress using a Diversity and Inclusion Maturity Model like the one that follows, reprinted with permission of Teagan Dowler, founder, the BCW.

Diversity and Inclusion Maturity Model

LEVEL	UNAWARE	COMPLIANT	STRATEGIC	INTEGRATED	DISRUPTIVE
Mindset	What's the point of D&I?	D&I has to be done, so we do it.	D&I is important to our success.	D&I is part of everything we do.	We're leading D&I best practice.
Organization	No desire to address D&I. No policies in place.	Addressed basic compliance requirements, basic data collected and standard policies developed.	D&I is a strategic objective for our organization. Key performance indicators (KPIs) are defined and tracked.	All policies and practices reflect and reinforce the D&I strategy. Organization actively supports underrepresented groups.	Organization ideologically supports D&I and demonstrates leading corporate practices in this area.
Leadership	Unaware/ uninterested in D&I. Maintain the status quo.	Doesn't own D&I. D&I responsibility with a select few, usually HR.	All leaders own and communicate the D&I strategy. Leaders are held accountable for D&I KPIs.	Leaders have strong D&I knowledge and integration across the business.	All leaders challenge their own bias and the bias in others.

Adapted and reprinted with permission of Teagan Dowler, founder, The BCW (www.thebcw.com.au).

A simple best practice to consider is adding inclusive leadership expectations to quarterly business reviews for all managers. The desired benchmarks and results should be explicit to help drive accountability. A few key aspects for business reviews would be for leaders to assess the composition of their teams in the areas of tenure, representation, development plans, promotions, resignations, and succession plans through a D&I lens. They should then be expected to outline how they plan to leverage strengths and address areas of opportunity relative to the analysis of their team dynamics.

As a business leader for more than a decade, I had the opportunity to apply these best practices as a part of how I conducted business. This analysis and planning shouldn't be viewed as a special initiative or relegated to a single member of the team. Instead, it should be viewed as a standard business practice and adopted as an integral part of how inclusive leaders view their business.

After ensuring that your organization is clear about the vision for D&I success, making inclusion a key element in determining salary increases and promotions sends the message that inclusion is part of the company's core values and conveys to every employee that the responsibility to create and uphold a culture of inclusion lies with him or her. In addition to being another way in which an individual stakeholder can contribute to overall profitability, it becomes a personal imperative.

MOVING BEYOND SMART GOALS

SMART (Specific, Measurable, Attainable, Relevant, and Time Bound) goals are commonly used as performance management tools. While SMART goals engage the mind and the hands—or the practical aspect of work—they rarely engage the heart, a key aspect of meaningful goal setting. Said differently, your D&I goals are SMART, aligned with your business, and appropriately incentivized, but does anyone care?

Whether we acknowledge it or not, our identities, experiences, and other matters of the heart are inextricably linked to the personae we present at work. In order to derive the most value from each member of a team, organizations must pave the way for their success through policies and practices that are mindful and have meaning to facilitate their wholehearted participation. To borrow from the classic movie *The Wizard of Oz*, we need brains, heart, and courage, too, to achieve our organizational inclusion goals. In the next chapter, we will explore ways to objectively see and hear what is happening in our organizations in order to get to the heart of what it will take to create a culture of inclusion.

CHAPTER 6

Open Your Eyes and Ears

*Sometimes we have to deal with the bad and
the ugly to get to the good.*

◆ *What do you see?*

◆ *What are you overlooking?*

◆ *What can you stop tolerating?*

Let's begin this chapter by opening our eyes and ears to "good."

Organizations of all types are adopting diversity and inclusion as part of their business strategies, primarily because a growing number of leaders in business, the nonprofit sector, and academia are coming to grips with two central ideas:

◆ Participants in their worlds—stakeholders, customers and clients, and employees—are likely to grow more diverse, and diverse in greater numbers, than in the not-too-distant past.

+ Diversity's benefits in the business world and beyond are increasingly well known and accepted, particularly since numerous studies around the world have confirmed those beneficial results.

Recognizing that an imminent tsunami of worldwide social and economic change threatens to drown their enterprises, leaders are deciding to ride the wave. They realize that achieving a sustainable competitive advantage demands rapid growth in this area, and therefore they are poised for change. The urgency of this need has shaped a message that is getting through to all those willing to hear it.

THE GOOD: CEOS WORKING TOGETHER FOR DIVERSITY AND INCLUSION

In the spring of 2017, a nucleus of 175 CEOs leading national and multinational corporations formed CEO Action for Diversity & Inclusion, a coalition designed to bring together leaders actively advancing D&I in the workplace. Now, just a year later, CEO Action represents more than 450 CEOs and twelve million employees.[1]

The reach and resulting influence of this collective is substantial and ever-expanding. What is perhaps even more encouraging about CEO Action is that in order to join, leaders must pledge to take three D&I actions:

+ support dialogue regarding complex and difficult conversations about diversity, equity, and inclusion;

+ educate with regard to unconscious bias; and

+ report the results of both successful and unsuccessful actions so that other organizations can benefit from their efforts.

The CEOs that are part of this network are all trailblazers operating at the vanguard of leadership. They understand that the current culture demands a commitment to D&I and a corresponding set of ever-evolving best practices.

From the perspective of a coach, I reflect on this group of dynamic leaders. I am curious about the driving forces that compel these CEOs to make such a public commitment. What gives them the fortitude to stand up and speak out? How do they push past resistance and barriers relative to diversity, equity, and inclusion? Most important, how do they ignite the same commitment to action in their executive peers? Opening our eyes and ears to how others are answering these questions can help coaches, managers, and D&I advocates alike spur more people in power to see the value in creating inclusive environments and make business better for everyone.

THE BAD: SUBTLE DISCRIMINATION IS DEEPLY ROOTED

One major impediment to achieving the kind of "welcoming, collaborative, and thriving environments" that groups like CEO Action aim to foster is a widespread tendency to neither see nor hear the ways in which diversity group members are subjected to subtle discrimination and microaggressions, which cumulatively nullify both their individuality and their humanity.

For instance, many people who are nonwhite, nonmale, or both have had the experience of attending meetings where they were the sole person who was not like everyone else there. If you are a member of the dominant majority, imagine what it would be like to attend a meeting filled with African-American, Latino, and Asian women when you are the only man present, and white besides. Then imagine what it would be like to have this experience almost exclusively throughout your career, not simply at one uncomfortable gathering you were forced to attend when your company acquired new business partners.

Can you imagine what it would be like if there were no white men on your company's board of directors and if every C-suite position were occupied by women of various nonwhite races? Any feelings of awkwardness and diminished power you may be experiencing approximate what has long been the experience of diversity group members.

What would it take for you to feel included in the group, for you to feel that they viewed you as equal and different? Because inclusion is not about turning a blind eye toward the ways in which other people are different. In fact, two of the most common microaggressions that diversity group members face are *color blindness* and *whitewashing*—that is, when a member of the majority group claims that they "don't see color" and holds their experience and way of being in the world as the expected standard. What they're really doing is minimizing the experiences of others that differ from their own, and it is a huge barrier to creating an inclusive environment.

Microaggressions can feel like water dripping on a rock—eventually wearing down even the strongest person if left unchecked. To avoid them, many people choose to wear a mask at work, embracing their authentic self and culture only after they close the door to their office on their way out for the day. Others decide to leave an organization entirely to find a workplace where they don't have to compromise or hide their identity. With the goal of elucidating the nature and impact of these everyday interactions, I will share with you one of the microaggressions I've personally experienced.

It was a day like any other when a colleague replied to an email I had sent our team. Along with her response, she included a question: "Why is your name La'Wana?" She had copied the other members of our team.

"My mother chose to name me La'Wana," I typed, and hit send, hoping my short reply would signal the end of the exchange.

But she and others kept the conversation going by asking why my name had an apostrophe. One colleague even suggested that I change my name. In other communications, they repeatedly misspelled my name, despite its being prominently displayed in my email signature.

Soon they were adding *La'* before their names when responding to my email messages. One of my team members later joked that she planned to change her name to La'Melissa. Some chose nicknames for me or called me by my initials, disregarding my name altogether. While their comments and behaviors may seem like fun and games or harmless jokes, they're not; these are prime examples of microaggressions.

Working with people from all over the world requires me to be intentional about how I spell and pronounce names with which I am unfamiliar. It also necessitates leaning into my cultural intelligence—and my personal experience—to understand that it is inappropriate to make jokes about, change, or alter a person's name. I am aware of the significance of family names in certain cultures—making courtesy and respect that much more crucial. In fact, many cultures around the world maintain deeply rooted values and beliefs about an individual's name being linked to his or her destiny.

In an interview with the *Improper Bostonian*, actress Uzoamaka Aduba shared the story behind her name: its meaning, her struggles with it growing up, and why she never considered changing it:

> *My family is from Nigeria, and my full name is "Uzoamaka," which means "The road is good." Quick lesson: my tribe is Igbo, and you name your kid something that tells your history and hopefully predicts your future. So, anyway, in grade school, because my last name started with an "A," I was the first in roll call, and nobody ever knew how to pronounce it. So I went home and asked my mother if I could be called "Zoe." I remember she was cooking, and in her Nigerian accent she said, "Why?" I said, "Nobody can pronounce it." Without missing a beat, she said, "If they can learn to say 'Tchaikovsky' and 'Michelangelo' and 'Dostoyevsky,' they can learn to say 'Uzoamaka.'"*[2]

Sometimes we put on blinders. Because of the way we live, we think we're fine, that we don't have a problem with women, people of color, or members of the LGBTQIA community. We think of ourselves as nice people just going to work and doing our jobs, just like Todd in the example below. Uzoamaka's story and her mother's simple wisdom highlight the fact that pressure to conform, change, or assimilate is not really about the difficulty of spelling or pronouncing a name, but rather about others' unwillingness to learn. It's a matter of choice to address our own biases, unconscious or not, and honor the cultural differences we encounter in one another—no matter how they appear.

COMBATING THE "GOLDEN COUNTRY CLUB"

I've coached many managers and leaders who feel diversity and inclusion has no bearing on their office culture or their organization's ability to innovate and succeed. As such, they pay little, if any, attention to D&I when hiring and developing company policies and procedures. In one instance during a group coaching session, Todd, a department manager, said that he never considered race, gender, or any other aspect of diversity when hiring. "I just hire the best person for the job," he emphatically declared.

Moments earlier, a colleague from outside his department had just revealed that Todd's team was known as the "golden country club" for its lack of diversity and boys' club vibe. This was not news to Todd—he was well aware of his group's reputation. In addition, he had heard others outside the department refer to his team as the "workplace fraternity," and now that he had the floor, he was explaining just how the demographics and culture of his team had come about and why they weren't an issue.

Just then, a newer member of Todd's team, Michael, spoke up. He shared that his wife had challenged him recently, stating that he was oblivious to the fact that all of his direct reports were white, heterosexual males between the ages of thirty and sixty—just like him. Not only were all of his direct reports members of that demographic, but the entire department was homogeneous and it had been that way for decades. Unlike Todd, Michael was beginning to see why this was an issue.

After the session, Michael approached me to request one-on-one coaching. He said that "things are pretty good around here," but after his wife's comment, he couldn't just maintain the status quo. She had been experiencing blatant gender discrimination at work, and he was deeply bothered by the realization that his team dynamics were strikingly similar to the ones at his wife's organization. After hearing about her experience, he had begun to understand how problematic it was. He was visibly emotional when he said, "I had to look my wife in the eye and admit that I've been contributing to the system that is causing her so much distress."

Michael wanted to explore ways to bring more diversity into the department, but he was apprehensive about how shaking things up would be received by his peers. Todd's resistance to acknowledging that his department had any issues was a perfect example.

There are several important takeaways from this story:

1. Organizations need to open their eyes and ears to the ways in which subtle discrimination and unconscious bias manifest themselves in the workplace. In this case, Todd didn't think he was exclusionary because he "doesn't see differences," but the makeup of his department told a very different story.

2. Sometimes we have to voice the bad to get to the good, and that requires creating a space where people feel comfortable sharing things they may not be proud of. Despite the current flaws in his department's culture, at least Michael felt comfortable sharing his concerns with his peers. Then later, coaching provided him a safe space in which to discuss the circumstances one-on-one, which opened the doors for positive change at his organization.

3. We must also call out the flawed thinking that hinders progress. If the Todd in our organization says, "I just hire the best person for the job," we should respond, "Great, that is exactly what we all want to do throughout our organization. Let's discuss how increasing diversity helps us ensure that we acquire and retain top talent." The unspoken truth in Todd's statement is that some leaders feel that hiring with a diversity lens means settling for less than the "best." That myth needs to be challenged and corrected with awareness and coaching to get to the source of the fallacy.

WHAT RÉSUMÉS REVEAL ABOUT BIAS

Unfortunately, unfair and unconsciously biased judgments can take their toll even before applicants step through an organization's doors for a job interview.

☛ Data supports the reality that prejudice and bias are evident from the moment that minorities submit their résumés.

Research conducted in 2016 by Katherine A. DeCelles, then a professor of business administration at Harvard Business School, along with several colleagues uncovered the fact that prejudice is hardwired into the applicant-selection process. When the study's 1,600 fictitious minority applicants submitted résumés that whitewashed or disguised their race, they received a much higher percentage of responses from potential employers (25 percent versus 10 percent). Perhaps worse, employers who appeared diversity friendly (equal-opportunity pledges were posted on their websites) were no less likely to discriminate and still gave preferential treatment to résumés of people with white-sounding names.[3,4]

"It's time," noted DeCelles, "for employers to acknowledge that bias is hardwired into the hiring system, and prejudice is clouding the screening of qualified applicants."[5]

Why do employers prefer candidates who seem white? In her TED Talk "The Danger of a Single Story," Nigerian novelist Chimamanda Ngozi Adichie offered an answer. Adichie spoke about prejudice and bias as stemming from a single, widely propagated story about any given group, and the "single story" that companies hear about minority candidates is that they will not be "a good fit."[6] And so, these candidates are penalized for a stereotypical narrative that probably has nothing to do with them.

Despite the plethora of trainings in unconscious bias and cultural competence available to hiring managers and talent acquisition, HR, and recruitment teams, we still see employment discrimination running rampant in organizations. But as we've established, instruction on its own rarely sticks, because it doesn't evoke any real investment on the part of the trainee. This is why I prefer the coaching approach to inclusion, which engages participants with powerful, emotion-provoking questions such as these:

◆ *What types of people relate best to you?*

◆ *What types of people do you prefer to interact with?*

◆ *What role does culture play when you interpret applicant behaviors?*

Asking these questions requires people to consider their own preferences—and potentially the prejudices and biases attached to them. It shines a light on their impact on the hiring process and the applicants who are ultimately chosen. When managers and hiring professionals become aware of their tendencies to choose candidates who seem to be like them, they can actively take steps to counter those inclinations.

◆ *Does the applicant remind me of someone I know?*

This is another powerful question that recruiting and hiring professionals can reflect on to help self-manage and become intentional about challenging bias in themselves and others. It requires them to explore whether an outside connection is unfairly swaying their perspective on a candidate. Those who strike them as more familiar and who evoke positive associations will receive an advantage, while those who seem foreign to them or rouse negative comparisons—no matter how arbitrary—are far less likely to get hired. Sometimes people charged with hiring are also triggered by particular aspects of a candidate's appearance that are connected to their biases. I've coached clients triggered by traits such as dreadlocks, tattoos, and heavy accents.

It is important to state that bias and triggers in and of themselves are not the problem. We all have biases and we are all triggered on occasion—our efficiency and even our survival depend on possessing these mechanisms for decision-making. However, we must recognize them for what they are. Bias represents our interpretation of positive and negative stereotypes and experiences; they are not universal truths. In the case of recruiting and hiring practices, these cognitive shortcuts often result in flawed judgment and, as the data demonstrates, unfair hiring decisions. Mastering the delicate balance of making generalizations that protect us while challenging bias and its potential to cloud our judgment is not an easy task, but it is possible—and necessary.

Finally, taking a peek into the future, we will have to keep an eye on technological advances. For those who think artificial intelligence (AI) will remove bias from the hiring process, there is actually growing concern regarding bias in AI across most business functions, including recruiting and hiring.[7] While AI offers promise for predictive analysis, it also has blind spots that can disproportionately affect women and minorities. After all, human inputs are at the base of AI, and if those inputs contain bias, so will the AI.

"The field really has woken up, and you are seeing some of the best computer scientists, often in concert with social scientists, writing great papers on it," says University of Washington computer science professor Dan Weld.[8] "There's been a real call to arms."

We can't coach computers, but at least we can coach computer programmers!

THE UGLY: WORKPLACE DISCRIMINATION AND HARASSMENT

The "bad" in diversity and inclusion terms is often only a number of degrees removed from the "ugly" because they both inhabit a spectrum of negative, disempowering beliefs and behaviors that all too easily overlap. For instance, jokes told at the expense of women and minorities can easily turn into behaviors that demean and degrade. That's because the underlying problem amounts to more than just hurtful words: it's seeing women and minorities as less than human.

All organizations have antidiscrimination policies, but that doesn't mean discrimination isn't happening, and the U.S. Equal Employment Opportunity Commission's annual statistics demonstrate just how frequently this disturbing behavior occurs. In 2017, the EEOC resolved 99,109 discrimination charges on the basis of retaliation, race, disability, sex, age, national origin, religion, color, equal pay, and even genetic information—and secured $398 million in voluntary resolution payments and litigation.[9]

"Despite the progress that has been made," said Jenny Yang, former EEOC commissioner, "we continue to see discrimination in both overt and subtle forms."[10] Obviously those antidiscrimination policies are not enough to deter undesired behaviors or—more important—drive optimal ones.

In a 2017 study conducted by VitalSmarts, a leadership training firm, and Honesty Consulting, five hundred participants reported that they had experienced discrimination in some form and that it left them feeling "unwelcome, excluded, discounted, or disadvantaged because of who they are" by virtue of "their race, age, gender, national origin, religion, physical or mental disability, medical condition, pregnancy, marital status, or sexual orientation."[11] As a result, their ability to fully engage with their job and to feel motivated, committed, and eager to advance within their organization was severely compromised, so much so that a majority also reported debilitating stress, frustration, depression, and helplessness. They'd found that there was no clear way to effectively counteract subtle discrimination. The discrimination they experienced took the following forms, among others:

+ Being pressured to conform and assimilate into the main culture, instead of being encouraged to express their uniqueness
+ Being interrupted, discounted, and denied credibility
+ Overhearing blatantly intolerant jokes that were later denied ("just kidding")
+ Being excluded from meetings and social events, and denied information needed to perform their job
+ Being subjected to unfair, distorted faultfinding
+ Hearing that they lacked "executive presence" or otherwise didn't fit in, although their performance was exemplary and they would be commended if they were white, male, and young[12]

AN UGLY STORY OF RETALIATION

Unfortunately, ugly situations occur in the workplace on a daily basis, and many people find themselves navigating the choppy waters of microaggressions as well as covert and overt discrimination. The following story captures some of the ways in which a workplace's ugly culture affects us all:

Jasmine was just getting started with her day when her phone rang. The voice on the line quietly asked, "Do you have a minute?" It was one of her former team members, Liza.

She quickly glanced at her calendar and saw that she had thirty minutes before her next meeting. "Sure!" she replied with enthusiasm.

Jasmine heard Liza sigh with relief. "Great, because I really need to bounce something off you." She could tell something was bothering Liza by the tone of her voice. Jasmine closed her laptop and took a deep breath to center herself so that she could be 100 percent present for the conversation.

As an experienced manager and coach, Jasmine knew how to start a challenging phone call: "What do you want to walk away with from our conversation today?"

"Well," said Liza, "I really need your advice on how to handle a situation that has just happened with my manager."

"Of course. Tell me more," said Jasmine. Liza had switched to a new team a few months before, and Jasmine knew it had been an adjustment for her.

Liza shared the troubling experience she had had at a recent offsite business meeting. Her manager and several of her colleagues had way too much to drink one evening while socializing after the meeting. In fact, her manager was so intoxicated that he did not show up for the next day's early session.

Liza sat in the meeting listening to the stories being shared by her all-male colleagues about their carousing until the wee hours of the morning. When she asked where her manager was, they all laughed and shared a few stories about his heavy drinking and what had ensued the night before, including that he had left the bar with a woman at around three in the morning.

But he's married, Liza thought. *His wife was at the holiday party just a few weeks ago.*

When two hours passed and her manager still hadn't arrived, Liza became worried. She decided to call security and have them go to her manager's room to make sure he was OK. The hotel personnel accessed his room and found that he was safe—just quite hungover. Liza was very relieved when the security officer assured her that he was fine.

When her manager finally arrived at the meeting an hour later, he smelled like a brewery. Liza's colleagues continued to cheer him on. It was a surreal experience for Liza, especially as a new member of the team. "It felt like I was in one of those fraternity party scenes in a college movie."

Jasmine paused before responding. She wanted to make sure that Liza was finished with her account. "That sounds like an awful experience, and, as I'm sure you know, it doesn't align with our core values as an organization."

She hoped her assertion could be of some comfort to Liza, though she knew that was probably unlikely—she considered herself to be someone who had seen it all, and this situation would have thrown her for a loop, too.

"Is there anything else that you would like to share?"

Liza was quiet for a while and then said almost reluctantly, "Yes, there's more. The last two days of the meeting were even worse. I was repeatedly questioned by my teammates and my boss about whether I was 'comfortable' with what had happened. I felt like I had witnessed a crime and I was getting interrogated to ensure that I wouldn't testify. I couldn't tell which factor I found more offensive—the inappropriate actions of my manager and my peers or their bullying actions to keep me quiet.

"My manager went as far as to say that he had spoken to all of the team members individually and they were all OK with what had happened. 'Everyone is just worried about you and concerned that you may have been offended. We know you are very religious,' he said."

"How did you respond?" asked Jasmine.

Liza replied, "I am an African-American female on an all-white, all-male team. All of the midlevel managers are white males. All of the senior and executive leaders are white males. From my point of view, there was only one way to respond if I wanted to keep my job."

"I respect your decision, but I also want to encourage you to consider speaking with your HR representative," Jasmine said.

"No way!" Liza exclaimed. "I have seen other minority employees reach out to HR or their manager's manager with very bad results. After they spoke up, they were almost guaranteed to have a target on their backs. Soon after reporting their concerns, they would develop 'performance issues.' I only know this because there are very few minorities in our organization, and we try to support each other through challenging situations. Meanwhile, I now have a target on my back even though I didn't even voice my concerns about the actions at the meeting," she said.

"Why do you say that?" asked Jasmine.

"Since the meeting, my colleagues have stopped communicating with me almost entirely. They stop talking when I come into the room. And they often laugh when I leave. Plus, my manager is all of a sudden making comments about me not demonstrating enough leadership—even though my sales numbers are excellent and I have been leading the virtual development series for our entire division."

"That's tough," Jasmine said empathically.

"That brings me to the reason why I decided to call you today. I just found out that my manager has been talking down my performance to upper management and HR. He told me that he has communicated his concerns about my performance and that this role may not be a 'good fit.' He also shared that a realignment of geographies was on the horizon and that my territory would most likely be absorbed by the surrounding areas.

"I am not sure what to do next. I don't want to go to human resources now because it will look like I am just sharing what happened because my performance isn't up to par. I don't want to leave the organization because—other than this situation—my experience has been pretty good.

"It is unbelievable how drastically everything has changed. I feel like I don't even work for the same company anymore," Liza said, her voice trembling.

The truth of the matter is that when we take a hard look at the ugly, there are rarely standard protocols or quick answers. Sadly, not many resources are dedicated to culturally competent leadership, either. And the really ugly truth is that those resources are so few in number because so few organizations have multicultural leaders.

Think about Liza's situation. Her manager and her peers were accustomed to working in a strictly homogeneous environment. If we step back from our individual opinions about their behavior at the meeting and consider what her colleagues' perspectives might be, they could easily imagine that they were just being themselves as usual. The only difference was that Liza was there to witness their "usual." So in their eyes, they were not the problem; she was. Things were as they had always been—Liza and her religious beliefs were what was at issue.

We can all relate to attending an event—personal or professional—where we've been uncomfortable due to the superficial or uninviting environment we find ourselves in, making small talk while strategically planning our graceful exit at the first available opportunity. While this sounds like the making of a great comedy scene in an office sitcom or an awkward in-law gathering from a movie, it is a constant dynamic for many of those who are not a part of the dominant culture—and, just as in Liza's situation, the consequences are often dire for those of us who are not part of the in group.

◆ *What would the Inclusion Coach in you do?*

HOW TO COUNTERACT THE BAD AND THE UGLY

Find a time and place for small groups to talk about microaggressions and other bias-driven interactions they've experienced. Women might talk about small slights and inappropriate offhand remarks. Racial minorities might want to discuss the barely acknowledged assumptions they've been repeatedly subjected to. White men may share a set of covert messages that have been aimed their way, too. The idea is to get all of these microaggressions and miscommunications out into the open, where they will stop harming people and can instead be addressed head-on.

By making the effort to see and hear the subtle and covert, as well as the obvious and overt, the two forms that deeply ingrained biases and discriminatory tendencies take, you remove the corresponding cultural veil of denial and avoidance. Once it's out of the way, the problems that discrimination creates become visible and clear. And only at that point can you begin to move beyond lip service, as we'll see in the next chapter.

CHAPTER 7

Move beyond Lip Service (Sharing Power Is Harder—and Easier—Than You Think)

We won't make progress until historically dominant populations come to grips with their willful blindness toward institutional oppression.

◆ *How do we harness the collective knowledge, influence, and, yes, privilege of society's existing structures to empower those in the minority?*

◆ *How can we support leaders who are willing to share their power to allow others to succeed?*

◆ *How do we recognize that for some members of the majority, replacing their colleagues with women, people of color, and other underrepresented groups makes them uncomfortable?*

Many of us view diversity through an American lens, focusing on the country's most prominent diversity issues, such as tensions between black and white communities and concerns related to immigration. To shake things up, I'm going to begin addressing the reflection questions above by considering a different geographic area with a fairly homogeneous population: Japan.

Do countries and communities like Japan face the same struggles regarding representation and power? The short answer is yes, as it turns out. In fact, many countries around the world with a variety of demographic configurations are attempting to figure out how to share power within their current constructs just like the United States. And like the U.S., they have their own set of struggles, as well as the goal of improving representation and creating the inclusive cultures necessary to maintain such an improvement.

THE PRIMARY DIVERSITY AND INCLUSION DILEMMA IN JAPAN

Japan is contending with a serious labor shortage: in the next twenty years, the country's workforce is expected to lose eight million laborers. And while carmakers were once the most popular employers for those with backgrounds in math and science, companies like Toyota—the world's largest automaker—are losing recent college graduates to jobs in finance and tech. To deal with the limited talent pool, industry executives are racing to bring on individuals from a once-untapped diversity group: women. They are offering scholarships, opening day cares, and hosting networking sessions to increase interest and access in what has long been a male-dominated field. But these companies still have a long way to go if they want to make a dent in the industry's gender diversity. Most carmakers in Japan have a dismal rate of representation: just 2 percent of managers at Toyota and 1 percent of managers at Honda are women.[1]

Meanwhile, at Nissan, where diversity efforts started back in 2004, a full ten years before Toyota and Honda launched their initiatives to hire more women, 10 percent of managers are women.

This indicates that real change is possible, though it will take work—and time—to get there.

Japan's auto executives cannot expect to hire a bunch of women and hope things will work out. In addition to creating supportive programs like day cares and flexible work schedules, asking powerful questions that address the concerns of both men and women regarding this demographic shift will help leaders decide where to focus their attention and ensure a more successful—and sustainable—integration process. Working with coaches, Japanese men can process their "male" experience while making the transition to sharing power with the women who are entering the workforce. Women can also benefit from coaching to help them make the transition into a male-dominated industry by reflecting on what they need to be successful and the interactions that harm or promote their productivity and inclusion in the workplace. Helping both parties process and adapt will allow these companies to achieve the long-term progress they so desire.

ACKNOWLEDGING AND ADDRESSING THE RESISTANCE TO D&I

A 2016 study was conducted to determine the impact of companies' pro-diversity messaging on the hiring process. Researchers created a hiring simulation in which half of the participants were offered recruiting materials that stated the fictitious company's pro-diversity position, while the other half received materials that were otherwise identical but did not mention its stance on diversity. Participants then interviewed for the "job." Their interviews were taped and evaluated by independent raters. In addition to their performance being gauged, interviewees were monitored for cardiovascular stress.

The study found that white men who had read the pro-diversity statements showed more cardiovascular stress and performed worse than those who had not. These responses appeared across the board for this demographic, regardless of the men's political opinions, attitudes, and beliefs about diversity and minority groups, indicating the intense, subconscious resistance to diversity among those who have traditionally held positions of power—even when they agree with and believe in D&I practices.[2] To white men, diversity and inclusion is perceived as a threat.

This reality manifests in a number of other ways, including members of the dominant majority making threats of their own when they're worried about losing ground. For instance, in 2016, Brian Krzanich, Intel's former-CEO, reported that he and his leadership team had been threatened with violence and even death because of their decision to commit $300 million toward increasing the company's diversity profile and providing more opportunities for women and minorities in tech.

Such extreme reactions are grounded in the fundamental misunderstanding that there is some conspiracy to simply replace European-American men with women and underrepresented groups. That is not the intention at all. The goal is to provide equal opportunity, access, and challenges to *everyone*. As Krzanich said at the 2016 PUSH Tech 2020 Summit in San Francisco, "We stand up there and just remind everybody it's not an exclusive process. We're not bringing in women or African-Americans or Hispanics in exclusion to other people. We're actually just trying to bring them in and be a part of the whole environment."[3]

We are trying to level the playing field. That said, due to a long history of unfair advantages, there will be a period of time when representation is at the forefront of D&I efforts to help correct course and establish a diverse foundation from which to build. And, yes, that does mean fewer white men in positions of power, but it does not necessarily mean a loss of power. We all have to acknowledge this and deal with where we are today in order to move forward.

DISMANTLING THE BARRIERS
TO SHARING POWER

There are critical keys to unlocking the next level of diversity and inclusion, especially as it relates to shifting the power dynamics away from the unspoken norms of company culture that may as well have been labeled "For white men only."

These are the factors that never make the corporate presentation slides but still serve as a company's *real* cultural norms and values. They are expressed every day in a multitude of ways, and everyone knows about them, but speaking of their presence is considered taboo. When they *are* discussed, it is in the form of whispers and murmurs, often behind the doors of an HR representative's office, and only when addressing a pointed complaint.

We know that it is time to throw open the coffers and harness the collective value of talent that lies in a diverse workforce, but doing so requires that we acknowledge the current state of our culture and where it came from. We can't just speak our truth, we have to *own* it. That latter part is the most important—and the hardest.

LET WHITE MEN OWN THEIR TRUTH

"I am a white male, and I know that we need to increase diversity and inclusion."

I'd like to see us build the kinds of environments that allow for more honest conversations that move beyond the standard lip service of such statements. Perhaps if this individual making the statement above were to present the totality of his truth, it would sound like this:

"I am a white male, and I know that *in theory* we need to increase diversity and inclusion. But the current power construct works for me. It has served me well, and I've had a thriving career. Honestly, I don't see what's so wrong with that; I'm very comfortable."

For the most part, we haven't made it OK for white men to make statements like that without blaming and shaming. But allowing them to tell their truth is a linchpin in the process of moving beyond lip service.

Why are statements like this so crucial? Because until historically dominant populations are able to come to grips with their blind spots regarding institutional oppression, we won't make real progress.

Society is rightfully calling out that not all positions of power can be occupied by white men; the future success of our organizations demands more diversity. But society can't fix things from the outside. Solutions must come from the organizations themselves, and especially those occupying the C-suite (i.e., white males). We must work from the inside out to make those in power comfortable with sharing it.

An important note: Some have misinterpreted the call to speak their truth or be authentic to mean that they can say whatever comes to their minds, no matter how offensive. To be clear, making derogatory remarks about any group regardless of the circumstances only perpetuates prejudice, bias, and exclusion. Moving beyond lip service involves more than just facing the ugliness of the past and the privilege of your reality. You must also present behaviors to address and undo their many negative effects.

HOW WHITE MEN CAN USE THEIR PRIVILEGE TO BUILD INCLUSIVITY

Men Advocating Real Change (MARC) is an organization doing great work to promote the involvement of men in diversity and inclusion work. MARC aims to advance gender equality, not in spite of but in partnership with men. The organization was founded on the understanding that those who traditionally hold positions of power are best positioned to make real change, and that these changes benefit everyone—men included. It also gives some great tips to help men use their voices to build inclusivity and increase their impact:

- *Stand for Equality:* Silence can be interpreted (or misinterpreted) as support for the status quo. When we are silent, those who exclude others feel that their behavior is justified, and those who are excluded feel marginalized and begin to believe that's "just the way things are." The best leaders let others know where they stand on issues of gender and inclusion.

- *Continue to Learn:* Good leaders stay committed to the cause and are open to learning how to become even more effective advocates for change. It's crucial to recognize that we all have more to learn, not only about the extent of inequality in and outside the office, but also about how to create the change we are envisioning.

+ *Share Your Stories:* Great leaders are always willing to share what they have learned with others. Using personal areas of growth as teachable moments is an effective way to gain broad support, and it is equally as important for personal growth to share our failures as it is to share our successes.

+ *Take Action Today:* Perhaps most important, effective leaders for diversity and inclusion seek out and create opportunities to act when and where they are. Leaders start discussions and initiatives for diversity and inclusion where they don't exist, rather than waiting to join them when they arrive.

ENGAGING THE POWER STRUCTURE MOVES D&I FORWARD

Most, if not all, executives work with a professional coach at some point in their career. As a coach or manager using coaching skills, you can provide white men, especially those occupying the C-suite, with questions to help them reflect on their position and privilege. Through this process, they can arrive at actionable diversity, equity, and inclusion goals that encourage them to share their power and benefit the entire organization as a result.

◆ *What is it like to be you?*

◆ *What scares you about diversity and inclusion?*

◆ *What do you choose to take responsibility for relative to diversity and inclusion?*

Give white men a safe space to own their truths and whatever resistance comes up. It may be awkward for them and for you, but whatever you do, let their comments stand without judgment. After all, the path to inclusion involves getting comfortable with the uncomfortable, as we will explore in the next chapter.

CHAPTER 8

Make Room for Controversy and Conflict (You *Can* Talk about This at Work)

Inclusion is not just about making everyone comfortable. Done right, inclusion will yield productive conflict and controversy.

◆ *What scares you about diversity and inclusion?*

◆ *What would it cost you if things remained as they are?*

◆ *What can you say no to?*

Difference is a fundamental part of diversity, and we've already discussed the myriad ways in which it is beneficial for business. Naturally, difference in opinions, beliefs, values, and more is also a recipe for conflict—and that can be a good thing! I believe that inclusion done right yields productive conflict and controversy and is the gateway to progress and innovation.

The operative term here is *productive*. When framed appropriately and addressed with curiosity, conflict can push organizations toward real progress, transforming the insights gleaned from moments of tension into critical steps in building sustainable solutions.

☞ What I would like to see is for leaders to create cultures that encourage their employees to effectively navigate and explore the conflict that arises from diversity instead of solely focusing on ways to avoid it.

PwC's 2017 "Diversity & Inclusion Benchmarking Survey" found that although companies are providing programs and building awareness of the need for greater inclusion through affinity, networking, and resource groups, they are not taking those efforts to the next level and using them to address business priorities. Could part of the issue be that companies fear the conflict that may arise if they do move to institute new policies and practices, based on the feedback they receive? And while more than half of companies track demographics, far fewer are measuring the factors that determine whether their environments allow for employees from minority groups to succeed at the same rate as majority-group members by looking at metrics such as discrepancies in performance, compensation, and promotions.[1] If they were to collect and analyze data on these factors, it would likely be clear that yesterday's solutions are not adequately addressing today's problems.

One reason corporations cite for failing to track or report this data is that they feel they could open themselves up to litigation, the ultimate conflict. If that's part of their consideration, it indicates that they're aware there is a problem. The core issue isn't that they're not sharing these metrics, it is that a disparity in performance, compensation, and promotions between demographics exists in the first place. Drawing the connection between *inclusion* and *innovation*—and introducing companies to the reality that conflict is part of the deal—is necessary in order to take all types of organizations and their stakeholders to the next level.

So what does it mean to make room for controversy and conflict in the workplace? It starts with talking about topics and taking actions that have traditionally been considered off-limits or taboo. It is acknowledging and accepting that, while ultimately beneficial for all involved, the process will not be easy or comfortable. Encouraging dialogue and corresponding action surrounding controversial issues will require people to move beyond their realm of comfort; it's like a company-wide stretch assignment. Bersin by Deloitte defines a *stretch assignment* as a task given to an employee that is beyond his or her current skill level in order help that person "stretch."[2] Likewise, creating an environment where all individuals are valued, respected, and empowered to do their best work requires us to stretch beyond our comfort zone and take the leap to build something new and better.

YOU *CAN* TALK ABOUT THIS AT WORK: RELIGION

In my coaching practice, numerous clients have shared their frustrations about having to hide their religious or spiritual preferences while they're on the job. A 2013 survey by the Tanenbaum Center for Interreligious Understanding demonstrated the prevalence of this sentiment, finding that one in three employees in the United States believes that employers do not accommodate religion in the workplace. To Tanenbaum's CEO, Joyce Dubensky, the study reinforces the reality that religion is a key aspect of diversity that needs to be embraced: "If there's one message from this survey, it's that religion is a workplace issue. . . . Employers who ignore it, do so at their own risk."[3]

While leaders may fear that engaging with what is often considered a touchy subject will bring about discomfort and even dissent, there are a number of ways to recognize and make room for religion without alienating employees. As a woman of faith, I remember reading a post on Berrett-Koehler Publishers' website in which the company's founder, president, and publisher, Steve Piersanti, discussed how he recognized the impact of this issue and found a way to express his own spirituality at work while making room for others to do the same—or not.

"During the first several months after BK was founded in 1992, at my request we began some company meetings with a prayer, but some BK employees expressed that they were uncomfortable with this practice. So we found an alternative that has seemed to work for BK ever since: begin certain company meetings with a short moment of silence (usually about a minute), which employees can use in any way they wish (meditation, centering, silent prayer, reviewing materials, etc.)."[4]

Not only did Steve create an environment in which employees felt empowered to share their discomfort with a pre-meeting prayer—an arena where conflict could be heard and registered—but then he modified the practice so that employees could participate on their own terms.

Steve went on to say, "I am grateful that we have found ways in BK to allow individuals (including me) to observe spiritual practices that are important to them—without compromising the rights or preferences of others."

Steve's approach provided flexibility to accommodate all types of individual beliefs. This is one of the reasons why I was drawn to his company and decided to publish this book with them.

While company-wide prayer sessions, inclusive or not, are something of a rarity in the corporate world, organizations can follow Steve's lead and provide accommodations that allow for religious and spiritual expression across the board. In fact, many high-performing companies are doing just that. Rev. Mark Fowler, the Tanenbaum Center's deputy CEO, notes that organizations are beginning to make adjustments, "crafting policies around religious accommodations, implementing quiet rooms, or starting a faith-based employee resource group."[5] By making room for a diversity of beliefs, these practices move beyond conflict and controversy and open the doors to real progress and potential. Next, I will explore a variety of ways in which organizations can begin to create environments that allow for all voices and experiences to have a place, and channel the conflict that arises productively.

SAFE SPACES

Organizational "safe spaces" allow people to share their experiences, speak their truths, and openly discuss where they are when it comes to diversity and inclusion—all with the goal of moving the needle forward. They can take many forms, such as employee resource groups, inclusion circles or councils, and individual coaching and coaching groups, all of which are explained below. The key here is that the purpose of these groups is more than just to have a space for venting; it is about finding ways in which the conflict that arises can inform insights that help create more inclusive environments.

Employee resource groups (ERGs) are voluntary groups within an organization comprising individuals who share identity characteristics or backgrounds—for example, women, Christians, LBGTQIA individuals, and African-Americans. ERGs offer an environment for people to come together and have conversations with people like them to help process their experiences and not feel so alone. They also provide a safe space for diversity group members to speak about issues they wouldn't necessarily feel comfortable addressing in front of a larger group. And that's OK. While the conflict and controversy that arise from a multitude of voices can be beneficial, people need to be empowered to move along their diversity and inclusion journey with multiple avenues for engagement. Inclusion is about maintaining individuality *and* being able to succeed within the larger community.

Inclusion circles are group meetings that serve as circles of trust for unfiltered dialogue where people can learn and grow together. Minority as well as majority group members are invited to talk about their positive experiences, painful moments, wishes, feelings, and overall thoughts and insights on working toward diversity and inclusion. Each participant is encouraged to repeat back to the speaker what they heard that person say, to be sure they are really listening deeply and engaging in a transformative dialogue without judgment. Interruption, cross talk, and responding with personal opinions are avoided.

Individual and group Inclusion Coaching is particularly useful in working with individuals whose actions show their resistance to D&I initiatives (regardless of what they say). In my professional experience and from talking with colleagues across industries and around the globe, most organizations have a decent amount of support from the top of the house or C-suite level, as well as from those on the ground level. The challenge often comes from the "frozen middle"—midlevel managers who say they are on board with advancing diversity and inclusion but do little to nothing to advance it. Research has also found this to be true. According to Jim Harter, Gallup's chief scientist of workplace management and well-being, somewhere between the top and bottom of an organization, "the understanding of and passion for an organization's mission drops by nearly 50 percent."[6] Coaches can give members of this vital segment the opportunity to self-reflect and own their truth, while encouraging them to engage in the conflict and controversy they would otherwise choose to avoid.

My advice is to employ a hybrid approach to making room for controversy and conflict that includes traditional ERGs for diversity group members, inclusion circles that bring together majority and minority group members, Inclusion Coaching for the "frozen middle" and other members of majority groups who would otherwise be left out of the D&I conversation, and an organization-wide **Inclusion Council** that aims to bring everyone together to move forward as a unit. The goal is to create avenues for "everyday" inclusion where everyone has a space that works for them.

Before moving on, I must address one of the potential derailers with "safe spaces." Some of the best-designed "safe spaces" can be undermined if they are not managed by the right people. I've seen well-intentioned plans be treated with warranted skepticism by employees who have been burned by untrustworthy gatekeepers—that is, leaders, HR personnel, and colleagues who promised confidentiality but did not honor their commitment.

It's a good best practice to routinely have a gut check for real versus perceived trustworthiness of the people who are in positions to conduct and facilitate tough conversations. If this is not happening, as an executive leader you could be perceived as aloof or, worse yet, "clueless" because you think everything is fine but in reality no one is engaging in meaningful discussions due to a lack of trust in the gatekeepers.

Keeping in mind the need for everyone to have a safe space at work, and the fact that there are many ways to accomplish this goal, we must accept the reality that there is no cut-and-dried solution here. As people, we'll continue to evolve, and so will the ways we address diversity and inclusion.

MAKE ROOM WITH A PAUSE

The creation of safe spaces is just the first step in making room for conflict and controversy. The much more difficult part begins once conflict and controversy is embraced, and you are then tasked with taking it to a productive place—before it devolves into chaos.

For this, I offer the PAUSE process for navigating and exploring conflict. It should be written into the ground rules of any group exploring diversity and inclusion issues and actively practiced during everyday interactions. When you or your employees feel a discussion has reached the point where you need to regroup, a few simple steps can serve as guideposts for reflection and corresponding actions.

First, **P**ay attention to what is happening without judgment, then **A**cknowledge your own reactions and interpretations, **U**nderstand how others' perceptions differ from yours, **S**earch for common ground to build productive solutions, and finally **E**xecute a mindful and intentional plan. This framework can help you steer things back on course when emotions run high and serve as a launching pad for reengaging in important discussions.

STEPS FOR A MINDFUL PAUSE

P Pay attention to what is happening without judgement.

A Acknowledge your own reactions and interpretations.

U Understand how others' perceptions differ from yours.

S Search for common ground to build productive solutions.

E Execute a mindful and intentional plan.

Adapted from Cook Ross Inc., lawanaharris.com.

No doubt there will be times when diving deep into diversity-related discussions that tensions rise and people default to their respective corners on an issue. This is just a part of the human experience when our assumptions and opinions are challenged. It's not an impasse. Having a process in place before you get to that point is critical, especially since we have historically been wired to avoid conflict. A well-defined—and practiced—process will support moving beyond the roadblocks that usually cause an abrupt halt in diversity and inclusion discussions. It is important to recognize when a PAUSE is needed, and since it should have been introduced in the ground rules, anyone can call for it at any time.

D&I 3.0?

If establishing a business case and building awareness is D&I 1.0, and establishing ERGs and unconscious bias or cultural sensitivity training programs is D&I 2.0, what is D&I 3.0? Could it be embracing controversy and conflict to address the root causes of resistance to diversity and inclusion in organizations? Will a generation of employee activists lead the way by bridging the gap between society and business? Will diversity and inclusion be seen as a business function, with D&I executives serving as business strategists?

I don't have a definitive answer for what 3.0 is—no one does yet—but an intentional effort to move beyond where we are today will help us discover the hidden treasures that lie within the controversies of our current reality. And once we can embrace the controversy that arises from diversity as a critical part of the journey, we will be more open to new perspectives that enrich our thinking and fuel our engagement in this critical business issue.

CHAPTER 9

Invite New Perspectives

---

*We can all decide to learn, study, and practice
new ways of thinking and doing that help us
change our behavior.*

◆ *Who are you becoming?*

◆ *What is possible?*

◆ *What will you do to stay aware of others' perspectives?*

These are a few questions to reflect upon as you think about yourself and the pulse of your organization. Is your corporate culture open and supportive to new ideas and diverse perspectives? Let's take a look at a few ways to help foster an environment that genuinely invites and values new perspectives—starting with who's at the table.

◆ *How do you know if there are a variety of perspectives at your table?*

If everyone agrees most of the time whenever there is a vote to be taken or a decision to be made, you probably don't. If you and I are on a team and we think very similarly, then one of us is not necessary in the room—and potentially at the organization.

Every employee is valuable human capital, and it is the responsibility of an organization and its leadership to maximize each individual's potential and contributions. Getting the most out of those we work with means changing the frame of the conversation and creating an environment in which everyone feels comfortable enough to contribute their unique perspectives—even when those ideas conflict with popular opinions.

Here's an example: When decisions are being made in a meeting, and business leaders are focused on the bottom line, financials, and cost savings, it is crucial to bring in someone who can add an additional layer of awareness, whether internal or external. With my background in human resources and global leadership development, I'll often address business decisions from a corporate social responsibility perspective, inquiring about their human impact. I'll ask the tough questions, such as how a layoff and restructuring the week of Thanksgiving might affect employees, and what a move like that might communicate to stakeholders in terms of how the company values talent. I'll ask how the decision might reflect on the company's reputation as a whole. Addressing these considerations can help the company avoid pitfalls, creating the potential for a better outcome even in tough times.

We need people to put out new ideas, others to challenge them, and still others to address them from a different angle. Different voices, different experiential backgrounds, and different ways of thinking are how we find ways to tap into new markets and expand our businesses. They help us understand why something we are doing today may not be working and offer new ways of operating that could be much more effective.

LEAN INTO CURIOSITY

My work as a coach and mentor hinges on the idea that when we become truly curious about the inherent value in every human being, we can build bridges that enhance all of our interactions, increasing our ability to be inclusive, to adapt, and to make meaningful connections. Those fully formed interactions often lead to the kinds of ideas that break the mold.

If leaders are curious about other people—how they think, the way they approach a task or challenge, and the manner in which they respond to particular situations—they can harness these unique insights to the great advantage of their businesses. Alternatively, if leaders have no desire to understand the different perspectives, values, and priorities of their team members, how can they provide meaningful guidance and support? How can they be truly effective leaders?

I add the qualifier *truly* to that last question because there are some leaders who show short-term success with narrow-minded leadership approaches. They micromanage their employees, are relentless in their quest for productivity, and do not care one iota about what their employees are feeling. It's all about the business. The even sadder reality is that there are still some senior and executive leaders who read that description and think that sounds like a good manager.

Suffice it to say, that is not the best way to lead a team for the long haul. Folks will burn out or quit long before any sustainable impact can be realized. These leaders are the ones that rise to prominence seemingly overnight with sudden success and then quietly exit the organization or find themselves in hot water with employee relations. I've seen several managers' careers derailed because they were not curious about different ways of doing things, let alone about people different from themselves. They operated with a one-track mind that ultimately led to their demise. In retrospect, it was like they could not get out of their own way.

☛ I encourage executives to consider embedding a healthy sense of curiosity in your core leadership competencies throughout your organization.

Doing so will encourage your leaders to find the value in others' perspectives. But first they have to invite those perspectives. This means moving far beyond compliance when considering inclusion and diversity, and creating environments in which everyone is encouraged to share their ideas, particularly when the ideas deviate from the norm.

Instead of becoming defensive, angry, or disengaged, lean into curiosity to try to understand why someone holds a different opinion or behaves in a certain, unexpected way. **It's pretty much impossible to be judgmental and curious at the same time.** I'm proposing that we really tap into our curiosity when things and people don't make sense.

Before we discuss how to solicit the kinds of voices and feedback that could help you avoid your next pitfall or land upon your next billion-dollar venture, I want to share a moment of cultural expansion—and inviting new perspectives—that I had the opportunity to be part of and that held major benefits for all parties involved.

At one point in my career, I relocated from North Carolina to Boston for my job at a large pharmaceutical company. My office was in Cambridge, a mecca for biopharma. I noticed that there was a large Asian population in my office building and in the area overall, and I became curious about my colleagues, not only from a professional perspective but also from a human one. I reached out to colleagues and set up lunches and dinners, and we eventually formed strong friendships. We swapped cultural stories and insights on cooking, travel, books, and more. I'm a huge proponent of alternative medicine, and we found common ground while discussing home remedies. They introduced me to various elements of Eastern medicine that I still use today. One of the most fascinating aspects of our exchanges for me was learning more about traditional Asian culture and cultural celebrations.

When December rolled around, I noticed that our office had erected an intriguing display. There were three white pillars, like the ones a bust would sit on. One had a traditional Christmas display on top, one had a menorah, and the third held a Kwanzaa display. This was the first time I'd seen any culturally related décor in our office. I asked one of my colleagues about it at lunch, and she said they put up the three displays every December. She mentioned that she wished there were something like that for Asian holidays.

We began to discuss the various Asian holidays, and she shared that she and a hundred other employees had been renting a restaurant to celebrate Chinese New Year for a number of years. Inspired by her stories and the camaraderie I had experienced with so many of my coworkers, I suggested that we do something to incorporate Asian holidays into the mix. We worked together on a proposal to bring the Chinese New Year celebration into the office, changing the date and focus of the event to celebrate the Lunar New Year, thus embracing a larger audience.

The organization approved and sponsored it, opening the event to all employees in the Massachusetts area. We decorated the office with Chinese lanterns and various aspects of Asian culture. There was even a choir of scientists that performed! A total of 207 people attended, and the celebration continues to happen on an annual basis.

Employee engagement and morale soared as we all relished the fact that the company chose to put resources behind a celebration of diversity and inclusion. My post in Massachusetts lasted only two years, but I maintain close friendships with many of the people I met while working and living there. None of this would have happened if I had not proactively sought to engage with my colleagues and learn about their experiences and unique perspectives. As you can see, the benefits of inviting new perspectives are both personal and professional.

HARNESSING THE POWER OF NEUROPLASTICITY

The remarkable potential to harness the power of the brain to create new ways of being debunks the myth that you can't teach an old dog new tricks, or in this case, you can't embrace new perspectives.

Scientists used to believe that the brain stopped changing after childhood, but we now know that the brain is not a static organ—it continues to shift and transform throughout our life. *Neuroplasticity* refers to the brain's ability to change—along with thoughts, habits,[1] and routines—through mindful practice and repetition.[2]

☛ While most professional coaches are not scientists, our work directly harnesses the principles of neuroplasticity: fostering the repetition necessary to create new behaviors and habits—and get rid of the old, unhelpful ones—in our clients.

In much the same way, managers and coaches can work with individuals to develop new, more inclusive behaviors that replace old, unhelpful, and biased ones. **The best part about the integration of neuroscience with coaching is that the change the client experiences is sustainable and replicable.** Once those neural pathways are created, they can be reinforced through repetition of the new behaviors.

Every time we think, feel, or do something, billions of pathways light up in our brain. Habits occur when we continue to repeat a particular action or way of thinking, establishing a well-traveled neural pathway that becomes our default over time. However, when we shift our thinking, learn something new, or invite a new perspective, our brain begins to form new pathways. As we use these new routes by thinking and behaving differently, new habits are established and the old pathways become weaker. This process of rewiring our brain to form new connections and rid ourselves of old ones is neuroplasticity at work.

As someone who majored in biology, I love the science behind it all. It forces me to reflect on just how powerful we are when we rely on the strength that can come only from within. We can all decide to learn, study, and practice new ways of thinking and doing that help us change our behavior. It is how we begin to transform ourselves and our organizations to truly embrace diversity and become more inclusive.

HONEST OPINIONS WELCOME

In order to invite new perspectives, an organization must establish an environment in which people are encouraged and rewarded for providing their honest opinions, even—and especially—if those opinions are counterintuitive or challenge the usual approach. There are many proven ways to encourage honest opinions and invite new perspectives, including employee-engagement surveys, as in the following example.

An international textile company recently conducted an employee-engagement survey with questions surrounding employee culture, leadership, and professional development. The survey was rolled out on a global scale, reaching the company's tens of thousands of employees.

Eddie Floyd, senior vice president of human resources at the textile company, was charged with evaluating and addressing the data with his team. He took a deep dive into the employee-engagement survey findings, curious about what the findings meant for the organization and its talent, and about what steps they could take to improve. He resisted the urge to cushion or explain away what could be perceived as negative feedback and instead saw it as a valuable gift that should be embraced and explored.

Actively engaging his curiosity allowed Eddie to rise above insecurity. He encouraged the managers who reported to him to do the same; however, reactions from the managers on his team varied broadly. Some were quick to say, "These results are not reflective of our department," in response to any feedback that could be perceived as negative. Others were open to all they heard.

Eddie seized this leadership moment by using coaching skills to ask powerful questions and create a space for judgment-free exploration and ideation. His approach led his team to a place of curiosity and understanding, rather than their going into defensive mode. Eddie then worked with his peers and his team to put in place action plans with prioritized, time-bound objectives.

As a result of Eddie's proactivity, stakeholders agreed that the survey was a worthwhile investment. Employees felt that they had been heard and that their input was taken seriously. Moreover, the engagement generated by the survey—and Eddie's openness to new perspectives—led to increased productivity and performance for the organization as a whole.

If Eddie hadn't taken his team's responses seriously, it would have demonstrated that he didn't value their feedback, and they might have been hesitant to contribute in the future. Instead, Eddie showed them that their opinions were important, encouraging them to offer more of their insights and ideas to help build upon the company's success. This level of leadership requires humility and vulnerability. Eddie's authentic invitation for, and receptivity to, all forms of feedback created a space where his team could tap into their resourcefulness and bring forward innovative solutions.

Other ways to invite new perspectives include holding feedback sessions, crowdsourcing opinions on internal social media channels, and using texting platforms for instant polling to address specific needs with short timelines. Technology's constant evolution creates endless possibilities for gaining new perspectives.

CREATING A JUDGMENT-FREE ZONE

In order to understand what others are trying to say—to listen without judgment—**we need to be aware of the filters we have that may affect what we're able to hear**. This awareness requires us to go deep within and deal with our truth. For instance, we know that we all have unconscious bias. How does that bias influence our ability to hear and process ideas from others? What filter do we place on ideas coming from a female, Latino, differently abled, or openly gay individual? These are just a couple of questions to consider when we are looking to maximize our ability to listen deeply.

The term *active listening* has been part of business communication jargon for years. We are told to listen to make sure we understand what is being said, to look at individuals when they are talking, and to paraphrase their comments to ensure the accuracy of our understanding. These are all important steps in grasping the meaning of what someone is presenting. But how do we listen to understand the impact that an individual wants to have, or even to understand the potential impact that his or her idea could have on the organization? And to take it a step further, how do we listen with an understanding of cultural differences and preferences?

If we approach every conversation with the belief that all individuals have inherent value—and the understanding that what they share could be key to the success of our team, or even the organization itself—we will pay attention accordingly. Listening deeply goes beyond making sure that you have heard accurately what someone has said; it's about the impact, the motive, and the intent.

Creating a judgment-free zone can lay the foundation for deep listening, as well as advancement and innovation. To do so, you need to set ground rules for yourself, your team, and your organization:

1. **Set the context for your conversation as one of authentic exploration, ideation, and brainstorming.** Let the group know that this is the time to share ideas, explore, and brainstorm. Let them know that you really want their honest opinions, regardless of how they think those opinions may land—and mean it. Lead the way by exposing some of your vulnerabilities. Reassure them that the conversation you are about to have is for opening up possibilities, not making concrete decisions or determinations.

2. **Remove the need for immediate action and open up the process to explore possibilities.** When I'm coaching a group that is very entrenched in its thinking, sometimes I'll raise the bar on the process itself and say, "Not only is this a no-judgment time of sharing, it's also a time when no actions will be taken." Then, that meeting—and that moment—is reserved exclusively for new insights and brainstorming.

   Without such parameters, once an idea is thrown out there, it's easy to jump in to explain why it can't work. But if we are too quick to come up with an answer or negate someone's perspective, it is impossible to really hear it. Instead, we've already applied our filters to it and come to a conclusion—sometimes before the person sharing has even finished speaking.

Knowing that action is off the table for the moment helps to remove some of the pressure to react immediately or to respond to a suggested change by saying, "This is the way we've always done it." **Don't judge, contradict, debate, or jump ahead. Instead, try to learn from what you hear.**

3. **Allow people to bring their whole selves to the table.** Cultivating an environment of curiosity empowers individuals to fully express their wholeness. Make it known that you want all individuals to bring the totality of their identities to the table. No one has to check part of him- or herself at the door or wear a mask to fit in.

☛ What cultural, socioeconomic, geographic, and even spiritual experiences can add a layer of richness and refinement to ideas and solutions, and yield tangible business results?

Tapping into the questions you may have about where the presenter is coming from and what he or she is truly saying will prevent walls from rising and help you gain a better understanding of another point of view.

Let's take a deeper look at the socioeconomic aspect. During my travels to Haiti and other countries around the world, I've seen people do amazing things with next to nothing. I've seen children build toy cars out of empty egg cartons and then make those cars move on their own using scraps of trash. I've also seen people fashion together motorcycle parts, pieces of furniture, and building materials to make modes of transportation. What valuable perspectives could come from someone who has cultivated this type of ingenuity by necessity throughout his or her life?

In fact, one key business area where these perspectives can prove extremely valuable is cost containment. I've spent countless hours in meetings and strategic planning sessions focused on cost containment. I take pride—not shame—in my humble beginnings because they help me offer viable cost-containment strategies, stemming from a time when I had no choice but to do more with less.

4. **Ask permission when addressing others' ideas.**
   By asking permission to share your thoughts, rather than immediately challenging a particular contribution, you've already let down a little of your guard, as well as someone else's. The next step is to add some qualifiers, framing your input as a request or a suggestion. That allows the person to whom you are responding to say yes or no, or to change or tweak your offering, further opening the door to collaboration and new possibilities.

EMBRACE THE UNKNOWN

We're all pretty clear about the things we know well. Let's explore what we *don't* know. To be truly innovative, our organizations have to be places where it is OK—even encouraged—to ask questions without having answers, to take risks, and to do things that have never been done before. What if, rather than expecting people to bring all the right answers to a meeting, we tasked them with bringing the right questions? From there, we determine what perspectives are missing around the table, what we need to be curious about, what truths are being revealed, and what we don't know that can help us and our business. Your organization will be poised to be more intentional about how you address—and assign value to—the diverse perspectives that are shared.

CHAPTER 10

Tell the Truth Even
When It Hurts

---

*We don't appreciate how risky it can feel
for people to speak up.*

◆ *What story do you tell yourself about people who are different
from you?*

◆ *When you talk to yourself about yourself, what do you say?*

◆ *What truth would you like to share?*

In coaching sessions, clients often release themselves from the need
to say what they *think* they should say and just let whatever comes
up for them naturally come out. I've heard clients make statements
like the following too many times to count:

◆ *I get along with everyone; I just don't understand why more
blacks don't apply themselves and strive for a better life.*

◆ *I don't know why women are still talking about equality. I mean, aren't we all equal already?*

◆ *All white people are racist; they just don't want to admit it.*

◆ *Most people who are poor remain poor because of their choices.*

◆ *If people are living in this country, they should speak our language.*

More often than not, members of the dominant majority make comments that reflect their belief that everyone has the same opportunity, and those who have not achieved the same level of success are to blame for their current station in life. They believe that this "diversity and inclusion stuff" is just an excuse for people to not have to work hard. But diversity group members have their own fair share of biases about people unlike themselves, and those come up in coaching sessions too.

Many of these seemingly insensitive musings are a product of systemic oppression, a concept that is pretty much what it sounds like: everything about our society, or *system*—from our laws and customs to the way power is distributed, generally accepted behaviors, and more—is meant to perpetuate the success of one group while holding others back. It affects the way *all of us* conceptualize the world, whether we know it or not.

While comments like these are of course hard to hear, it is remarkable to witness clients recognizing and owning the fact that these are actually their beliefs for the first time. Doing so serves as a pivotal point in their transformation. Why? Because it is only when they answer these powerful and challenging questions honestly from within that they can begin to address those beliefs.

Coaching is like a two-way street. The experience is equally impactful for the coach. Witnessing the vulnerability and raw truth that arise out of this process can be a powerful experience for coaches as we navigate our own personal and professional journeys, and sometimes those experiences are painful. I remember coaching a gentleman I'll call "Tom."

Tom was on a senior leadership team with a large, multinational organization. He and his team were having some serious interpersonal issues, and he had reached out for help meeting his professional goals. Tom shared that he felt his team both undermined his authority and denied him credit and recognition for his contributions. He believed the treatment was due to the fact that he was the only person of color on his team. After sharing his beliefs, as well as his goals for the session, he paused and asked, "Can I just be real with you?"

"Of course—this is your session. What would you like to say?" I responded.

"I wish black folks would get themselves together and stop wearing dreads and walking around with their pants hanging down around their ankles—then we could get some respect."

Now, I have to be transparent about my internal response to hearing the whole of Tom's truth: I was triggered by his comments. I know all too well that this kind of thinking is yet another product of systemic oppression meant to keep the system in place: Rather than blaming the true culprit—the oppressor—the oppressed blame themselves. Tom felt that the opinions he and others had about black people in general were overshadowing his ability to be respected as a leader in his organization.

While I am not proud of it, a part of my truth is that for a quick moment, I judged Tom based on his comments. I kept my composure, but my inner voice was saying, "Never mind Inclusion Circles, I need to host some WOKE-shops around here and help Tom out of the sunken place."

I quickly and silently acknowledged that I was triggered, owned my internal reaction to the situation, and chose to remain present so that Tom could continue. The entire process took less than thirty seconds, but it was necessary for me to be honest with myself in order to best serve Tom.

We all need to be aware of our triggers, especially as coaches. We all have them, but not all of us know how to recognize them and react accordingly. Often, we give ourselves the benefit of the doubt and assume that we are always in control of our responses and actions. Leaders have to discipline themselves in the same manner when triggered by their employees, or even by certain environments. If we don't recognize our triggers, we are more likely to act based on our own internal filters and forget that the session or meeting is about the person, group, or goal we're working with, not ourselves.

For this reason and many others, I also recommend that diversity and inclusion be a core competency for professional coaches. How can we as coaches help people along their D&I journey if we have not done the internal work for ourselves?

EXPLORING THE "WHY" BEHIND OUR BIASES

If we are completely honest, we all like some people more than others. And while it's not politically correct to say so—especially not in the workplace—we may also like certain groups of people more than others, usually people that are most like ourselves. While likability is important to everyone when building relationships, Inclusion Coaching can allow individuals to look deep within to explore the core beliefs from which this propensity to like or dislike originates. Is it based on previous experiences, a lack of familiarity, or a single story? And what is the potential impact if we make a decision based on likability versus more objective information?

Without this additional reflective lens, it is easy to default to placing blame or excluding those we think we just don't like, completely excusing away any bias or isms that may be the true culprits. As essayist Hannah Moore wrote in 1881, "The ingenuity of self-deception is inexhaustible."[1]

Honing the skills to diagnose your own attempts at self-deception, as well as others'—and seek out truth instead—may be tiresome, uncomfortable, or even painful, but it's essential when promoting diversity, equity, and inclusion. This will require a level of radical truth and vulnerability that we have yet to achieve—but it's possible.

Let's say your team is composed of only white men. Or maybe your team does have some diversity, but it's not really being leveraged. You may find yourself making a number of excuses for not taking a proactive approach to increasing your team's diversity or truly harnessing the diversity you do have. Maybe you just started at the organization, and you imagine that this is just the way it is—why rock the boat?

You know your team would be even stronger if it were more diverse, or if the diversity you do have were better utilized, so why don't you want to rock the boat? What is the "why" hiding behind your reasons for not acting? What story are you telling yourself about why it's better to keep quiet? What truth should you share instead? This is the kind of self-reflection that will eventually empower you to speak up and move the diversity and inclusion conversation forward.

WHAT IS YOUR ORGANIZATION'S TRUTH?

Truth telling must occur on an individual *and* organizational basis for real diversity and inclusion to proliferate. Let's explore the workplace reality of a millennial we'll call Eric. He offered a different take on the classic party metaphor that is often used to describe diversity and inclusion and the kind of organizational truth telling that needs to happen in order to move the needle:

> *Let's imagine you are throwing a party for your friends. You've tailored the entire experience to fit the needs and desires of those attending. Everything from the food to the music to the décor is pulled together with that group in mind. After putting all of this together, you let your friends know that they can invite anyone they like. You extend an invitation to your neighbors and a few of your coworkers, too. It's party time, and you and your friends seem to be having the most fun. You guys are loving the food while singing and dancing to all of the songs.*
>
> *The other guests seem to be having a harder time getting into the party, though. At first glance, you might say that the*

guests are being a little rude by not adjusting their mood. You may ask yourself, "Why aren't they having as much fun as we are? This is a nice party! Anyone should be able to have fun here."

This is what most work environments are like. The organization's structure, policies, and culture have all been formulated with a specific group in mind. Unfortunately, all of the individuals who decide to work for your organization won't fit into the group you originally designed it for. It's your responsibility to reimagine and redesign your organization to create a comfortable environment for all of your employees. We must go beyond simple "inclusion" work and venture into the work that reforms and disrupts.

To do this, I feel we must ask some tough questions:

+ How might our policies be complicit in systems of oppression?
+ Whom do our policies benefit most and why?
+ What can I reimagine about my business to create a more versatile experience that fits the needs of all my employees?
+ How might our professional expectations be predatory and discriminatory toward certain groups of people?
+ How can we create opportunities for marginalized groups to thrive?
+ How can we affirm people's true identities—beyond their utility at work?
+ What do people need from us that goes beyond a paycheck—and can we provide it?

If your organization is unaware of the impact and reach of systemic oppression, it is undoubtedly participating in the perpetuation of that oppression. This is where our discussions must begin from now on.

Unless you've been in a cave for the past ten years, you've seen the data that shows the pivotal role that millennials play in the future success of organizations. And make no mistake: They are taking note of the organizations that walk the talk relative to inclusion. Millennials—44 percent of whom identify as nonwhite—now make up 53.6 percent of the workforce, and as the world's population becomes more diverse, the window of tolerance for a culture lacking in inclusion and plagued by isms is going to narrow even further.[2]

Your organization as a whole needs to be aware of its truths and the excuses it makes. If you're not showing real D&I progress, if engagement surveys demonstrate that people do not feel a sense of belonging, if you're not able to attract and *retain* diverse talent, then what are your organizational truths and what are your excuses? If you don't know, it's time to find out, and that will require you to take a long, hard look at yourself and everyone around you. To demonstrate what sharing your truth can look like, I'll take the lead and share mine—unfiltered.

CHAPTER 11

My Truth, Unfiltered

*I'm not concerned about the truth that
makes me free; I'm in pursuit of the truth
that makes us all free.*

My father was a retired military combat engineer who was laid to rest at Arlington National Cemetery. I love my country, and I have the deepest respect for all who serve in the armed forces to protect our freedom. My mother is a scheduler for a large health-care system, and she is a pillar of strength for my family. My husband and I live in our home state of North Carolina, as do our three adult children and our adorable grandson.

I've had enriching professional experiences working with several large multinational organizations throughout my career. I have pursued my lifelong passion to promote social justice by volunteering with nonprofits whose missions are close to my heart, and I've had the privilege of coaching, mentoring, and counseling thousands of people. I am grateful to have found so much meaning and fulfillment, both personally and professionally.

That said, my family and I are not immune to the constant reminders that we are African-American, and that some consider that to be a detriment, or even dangerous.

I have been called the N-word. I've been followed by clerks while shopping in department stores. On one occasion, my husband and I were pulled over for no apparent reason. It was the middle of the night, and on the shoulder of the highway in the dark, the trooper told my husband that he had stopped him because "You looked like a suspect we have a warrant for."

I mention these troubling experiences—and the reality that they are commonplace for people of color in America—as a backdrop for our discussion about the workplace. Nothing happens in a bubble. As a person of color—whether I'm at my local mall or in a meeting of senior executives—I am always made aware that I am different.

Difference, at face value, is not a problem; we've seen the numerous ways in which it is often an asset. The problem arises when that difference is viewed as a deficit.

I want to share some of the experiences I've had during my career in order to shed light on the derogatory comments and behavior many people of color and members of marginalized groups endure on a daily basis at organizations around the world. My hope is that those who have experienced similar treatment will know that they are not alone in their quest for inclusion, and that their perceptions are not only real, but also bolstered by robust data from multiple sources spanning several decades.

I also want everyone to understand the consequences of exclusion, as well as the inherent value in appreciating our differences. Finally, I want to help create a future in which my grandson is not judged, overlooked, or devalued because of the color of his skin. Together we can draw on our collective experiences and perspectives to work toward a more inclusive mindset in our organizations and in our society at large—and harness the vast potential of that mind-set for the betterment of all.

THE ONLY ONE

Over the course of my career, I've attended thousands of meetings, team activities, and social gatherings. Most of the time, I am the only African-American in the room. For years, I was the only woman as well.

I will never forget an unfortunate incident that occurred at a meeting for district sales managers. I was part of a group composed entirely of white males—the only African-American and the only female. After presenting our regional director with our business plans and growth strategies for the next year, we all went out for dinner together. While we were chatting as we waited to be seated, one of my colleagues turned to me out of the blue and said, "You were very articulate in your presentation today. Now come on and talk some Ebonics for me; I know you can do it."

I excused myself and went to the restroom to regroup, hurt and angered by his remarks. I did not address his comment when I returned, and instead continued chatting as if nothing had happened. If something like that happened today, I definitely would have responded, but at that time in my career, I was not ready. I hadn't found my voice yet.

That Ebonics comment is just one example of the microaggressions that I have encountered in the workplace, and there are many subtler examples from interactions with people who have had little or no exposure to people of color. For example, I cannot count the number of times that I have been called "girlfriend," "girl," "sister," or "homegirl" at work—and never by a person of color.

☞ It is always important to demonstrate a high level of emotional and cultural intelligence when interacting with people unlike yourself.

I encourage those working with "only ones" to consider what their colleagues' experiences may be like, if they haven't already. If you have had limited experiences with people of different backgrounds, the best way to engage them is to have a genuine conversation, rather than assuming you understand where they are coming from or what their experience may have been. Consider asking them to lunch or coffee so that you can get to know each other better and cultivate mutual interest and understanding.

I often wonder if my white colleagues have ever been an "only one" at some point in their lives, or if they have ever considered what it would be like to come to work as the single white person in their department for decades.

IT'S JUST HAIR

After twenty years of using harmful chemicals to straighten my hair, or wearing wigs to work in order to achieve what many corporate entities consider the "most acceptable" professional appearance, I decided to wear my natural hair. I was so tired of hiding my hair, eschewing my desired look, and limiting my self-expression.

I remember the overwhelming sense of release and liberation I felt as I drove to the hair-braiding shop to get some simple micro braids. I went in and asked the stylist for "professional-looking" braids, and I felt happy and confident that I had gotten what I asked for. But I quickly learned that, for many of my colleagues, there was no such thing.

I went to work with my braids, and you would have thought that my hair was on fire based on the looks that I got. People of color reading this can probably guess the infamous and all-too-common question I was asked all day long: "May I touch your hair?"

"I'd rather you didn't," I responded, with as much kindness and empathy as I could muster.

While I knew to expect this type of cultural insensitivity, I was still surprised by my colleagues' willingness to comment on my appearance—and even touch me—in the workplace.

I kept the braids for a few weeks but then returned to my "assimilation hair" to avoid the constant onslaught of cultural faux pas—well-intentioned and otherwise.

While the topic of how a person chooses to wear their hair may seem trivial, it's not. If you were to ask African-American women about their hair as it relates to their professional experience, you would likely hear about a constant struggle with internal and external critics. Many have been told that their natural hair is not professional. Some have been told that they would have more opportunities to advance if they straightened their hair, dressed less ethnically, and modified their communication style. These suggestions signal the pressure to assimilate into the dominant culture in order to succeed.

ASSERTION OR AGGRESSION

In my work as a leadership-development professional, I have completed numerous personality profiles. All of them confirm my preference for a direct style of communication and interactions. Yet for years I felt that I was constantly walking on eggshells regarding how I expressed my opinions, and I would often suppress my preference for direct interactions in order to avoid the "Angry Black Woman" stereotype. I didn't want my passion for excellence to come off as demanding or confrontational. This dynamic inhibited my authenticity and was quite exhausting, especially in a mostly homogeneous culture.

Fast-forward to today, and I have experienced some much-needed transformation. I don't know if it's the realization that I have more years behind me than ahead of me, if it is just maturity, or if I'm just tired of playing the game. Whatever the catalyst for change has been, I've reached the point where I don't fear speaking my mind for the benefit of myself, others, or the business—the manner that works best for me.

The unfiltered truth is that for a black woman living in America, there's a lot to be angry about, and being angry is not a bad thing. Everyone gets angry. The real problem is the miscommunication and miseducation surrounding cultural differences.

For example, from the moment I stepped off the plane on my first mission trip to Haiti, I remember wondering, *Why is everyone so angry and yelling at each other?*

But then after being more intentional in my observations, I saw that they would yell, point their fingers, and then burst out laughing in a moment of pure joy, before patting one another on the back or shaking hands. I quickly discovered that what I had prematurely judged as anger was really just a cultural nuance in Haitian communication preferences. My lack of familiarity with Haitian culture led to my own biased response. Takeaway: it's not always just a black and white issue or about minority versus majority misalignment.

That said, where the black-versus-white or minority-versus-majority dynamic does come into play is when similar behaviors are perceived, judged, and acted upon differently for these different groups. I recall a leadership meeting where regional directors were tasked with presenting their strategic plans for the next year, and the group would provide its feedback. During the session, an African-American director shared his plan. He was passionate and animated during his presentation, and when it was time for the group to provide their on-the-spot feedback, they roasted him. Though they recognized the quality of his content, they told him how over-the-top his delivery was, and his vice president spent ten minutes tearing apart each aspect of his presentation and berating him solely based on his demeanor.

Ironically, a white director presented later in the meeting, and his delivery was much more boisterous and animated. He even used some colorful language. I remember bracing for the feedback after what had happened with the black director earlier. But instead of berating him, the group celebrated him for his passion and tenacity. That was one of my early experiences in how the rules shift for those who do not belong to the majority. And although that happened fifteen years ago, it is still happening in organizations around the world. The players may change, but the game is still the same.

My role in all of this has evolved over the years. I am no longer content to settle for being less than I can be to make others comfortable by participating in a social construct that is based on bias and isms. Instead, I work to help others differentiate between the inclusive workplace norms that should be embraced and the oppressive pressures to conform to systemic bias. These pressures can impact not only our work experience but our life experiences as well.

NAVIGATING A BICULTURAL
LIFE EXPERIENCE

Ella L.J. Bell Smith, a professor at Dartmouth's Tuck School of Business, researches race, gender, and social class in organizations. She documented the impact of having to hide one's true self at work in a study titled *The Bicultural Life Experience of Career-Oriented Black Women*. She found that those she interviewed "perceive themselves as living in two distinct cultural contexts, one black, and the other one, white. The women compartmentalize the various components of their lives in order to manage the bicultural dimensions. In addition, they tend to have highly complex life structures to embrace both cultural contexts."[1]

But black women are not alone. Many people of color face similar pressure to assimilate in the workplace. A 2012 report from the Center for Talent Innovation (CTI) titled *Vaulting the Color Bar: How Sponsorship Levers Multicultural Professionals into Leadership* demonstrates that people of color frequently feel the need to forgo authentic self-expression at work: "More than 35 percent of African-Americans and Hispanics, as well as 45 percent of Asians, say they 'need to compromise their authenticity' to conform to their company's standards of demeanor or style."[2]

In an early CTI report on the same subject, an Indian senior manager said, "You lead a dual life, you absolutely do. There is an inhibition. You just don't want to talk about it."[3]

If you have never experienced it, imagine what it would be like to be told that your appearance and identity were inherently unprofessional, and that in order to be successful, you had to cover it up or alter it. How would that feedback affect your ability to contribute to your company and your interest in doing so? How would it limit your potential, and the capacity of your team and organization to be truly innovative? Most important, what could you do about it?

The answer: for those in a position of power, use your privilege as a platform to promote an antidiscriminatory environment.

When you notice practices that are based on unreasonable expectations for assimilation, call them out and address them. Yes, there has to be a standard for operating an organization relative to cultural norms. I'm talking about those policies and even informal pressures to meet a fictitious standard set by the majority to perpetuate systemic bias.

Many of those in leadership positions have benefited from the support of their peers. Take, for instance, a senior director of marketing who is well liked by his colleagues and his direct supervisor. Accordingly, his name is mentioned repeatedly in conjunction with ideas that are viable and worthwhile. Eventually, he will attract the attention of higher-ups who can help him by nurturing his career. They'll give him career advice, offer mentoring, introduce him to people who can keep an eye out for appropriate opportunities, include him in meetings attended by a select group of people, and so forth. With all of this support, he'll be able to fulfill his potential and ascend through the ranks of his company.

But I coached a senior director of marketing, Anya, who had a very different experience. When she came to speak with me for the first time, Anya, an openly transgender female, was extremely frustrated. She did not receive the kind of acknowledgment and support that her male peers did during meetings and conference calls, and she was sure that those in the uppermost echelon of her company didn't even know her name. To add insult to injury, she was frequently expected to produce work that others were not the least bit ashamed to take credit for. As a result, it appeared that she contributed very little to the "work product" effort, and she'd not been offered the kind of assistance and, later on, promotions that members of the preferred group received.

Despite her frustration, she said she was ready to move on. "I don't want to hold on to those emotions," she told me. "I just want to prove that I'm good at my job."

"Well," I said, "what if you did hold on to them for a moment? Could there be value in that?"

She looked at me, unsure of what to do next.

"Take a moment and explore what you're feeling," I urged. Together, we worked through her full experience of being marginalized by not shying away from the emotions associated with unfair treatment. She resisted the urge to push past her anger, hurt, and frustration, and instead embraced the shadow that had been cast over her work environment. She had a transformative experience as she reclaimed her power to choose how she showed up in the incidents that were happening.

She decided to confront the instances of marginalization, microaggressions, and racism head on, and began speaking up. Anya was surprised to find that a couple of her colleagues were open to learning about her experience and receptive to confronting their own discriminatory behaviors as well.

During our next session, she was elated to share that one of her colleagues spoke up to support her during one of their teleconferences. Anya had voiced an idea that received no recognition from the group. Later, one of her male peers offered up the same suggestion, and the call's host said it was "perfect."

Her colleague jumped in. "Yes, I think that's an excellent suggestion—Anya actually mentioned it earlier." The meeting's host immediately apologized and thanked Anya for the contribution.

Anya's colleague's action was an act of antidiscrimination: he took the steps to actively counter the bias and diminishing tendencies of the group. When done consistently, acts like this one help to reframe expectations for fair and equal treatment, and work to ensure that credit is given where it is due.

I share these experiences as an integral part of my story to encourage you to hang in there when times are tough. You never know when the things you are going through today will allow you to help others who find themselves in similar situations in the future.

BRINGING MY AUTHENTIC SELF TO WORK EVERY DAY

I've made my choice after living the good, the bad, and the ugly in my personal and professional lives as it pertains to diversity and inclusion. **I'm ready to live unapologetically, free from internal and external critics that want me to play small for others to be comfortable.** I am going to use the rest of my professional career to advance diversity, equity, inclusion, and belonging in the workplace and in society. Most important, I'm going to help as many people as I can who are facing unfair treatment and oppressive work environments by sharing my truth while encouraging them to do the same.

Many companies have a "Bring Your Child to Work" day, an opportunity to show children what their parents do all day and introduce them to the professional possibilities that lie ahead. What if organizations held a "Bring Your Authentic Self to Work" day, an opportunity for employees to arrive as their authentic selves, without the filter of assimilation? Some people might not recognize colleagues they've worked with for years.

Experiencing the full expression of employees and colleagues while celebrating their uniqueness has innumerable advantages, from personal fulfillment to professional success and overall profitability—there's something in it for everyone, as I will explain in the next and last chapter of this book.

What's in It for Everyone:
Where Inclusion Can Take Your
Life, Your Career, and
Your Company

Experiencing the full expression of employees' and colleagues' identities affords us innumerable advantages, from personal fulfillment to organizational profitability.

While we've covered many aspects of diversity and inclusion, there are far more left to explore. D&I is an ever-changing dynamic of the human experience. As we wrap up our time together and you set out to improve diversity, equity, inclusion, and belonging in your workplace—and, hopefully, in your life—you'll encounter a wide variety of situations that will require you to draw and expand upon the considerations highlighted here. One key mind-set shift that will help you effectively incorporate D&I into your organization, career, and life, no matter what inclusion-based issues arise, is to focus on the WIIFE: what's in it for everyone.

WHAT'S IN IT FOR ORGANIZATIONS

We know that diverse organizations surpass their more homogeneous counterparts on virtually every level, from performance to profitability. The research, company stats, and real-life examples we've covered here demonstrate both the pros and pitfalls that correspond to inclusivity and a lack thereof, respectively.

First off, we've seen that, despite companies' copious D&I lip service, there are many barriers to true diversity, equity, and inclusion—most of them stemming from an old-school mind-set further limited by a lack of diversity at the top. These barriers also hinder success in a multitude of ways, and many companies are paying the price financially. Think back to those Equal Employment Opportunity Commission charges—99,109 of which were resolved in 2017 alone, costing private and government employers more than $398 million.[1] On the flip side, a study conducted by Bersin by Deloitte found that inclusive organizations were six times more likely to be innovative, six times more likely to be able to anticipate and respond effectively to change, and twice as likely to meet or exceed financial targets, compared with their exclusionary counterparts.[2] Another important benefit of striving for greater inclusion is that it pushes companies to cultivate emerging markets they might otherwise have ignored, and to approach those markets in innovative ways that could lead to insights and strategies that ripple throughout all areas of the business.

American Express, which broadened its outreach to LGBTQIA customers alongside its inclusive policies for employees, experienced these benefits firsthand. The company's chief diversity officer, Valerie Grillo, explained to *Forbes* magazine that the company knows just how much organizational inclusion pays off when it comes to recruitment and retention, as well as to customers and merchants. Regarding recruitment and retention, Grillo said American Express strives to be "an employer of choice," and she pointed to the company's high ranking for "LGBT-friendliness" and its "receptiveness [to] working mothers," a factor that nets them even more diverse, highly qualified talent.[3]

While internal inclusiveness has had an indirect positive impact on American Express's bottom line, its efforts to bolster its inclusive reputation among customers and merchants directly has affected its revenue. Hoping to build relationships with diverse customers and the merchants who sell to them, American Express has worked to further its reputation as an LGBT-friendly company, conducting a multiyear pilot outreach initiative for LGBT customers in Provincetown, Massachusetts, beginning in the summer of 2012. After handing out literature about the company's LGBT-friendly recruitment policies along with a list of merchants accepting their card, they saw a double-digit increase in charge volume. They also expect "diverse talent" from the LGBT community to become interested in working at American Express, based on their customer-outreach efforts.

This company-wide action started, of course, with people— as all major moves do. Organizations must delve beneath the superficial layers of engagement and get to the heart of their D&I matters by engaging the humans behind the business—and, as I've attempted to drive home in this book, that means the minority *and* majority group members.

The journey starts with a long, hard look in the mirror, identifying organizational truths, listening to the pulse of the workforce, and cocreating a path forward with employees across all levels in the company.

WHAT'S IN IT FOR YOUR CAREER

Considering that we end up spending a large amount of this one life we have to live at work, it is important that we figure this diversity, equity, inclusion, and belonging thing out for everyone's sake. We all win when we come together with pure hearts, open minds, and united spirits. It is not about creating a drum circle in the lobby of your office and singing "Kumbaya"; it's about doing the work we love with a great group of diverse, talented individuals. It's feeling good about bringing our authentic selves to work every day. It's about being more engaged, more productive, and more innovative.

Having people who think, act, and perform differently from you helps you grow and expand your ability to contribute more broadly across your organization. Your ideas can become more refined and relevant when the views of others—especially opposing views—are there to challenge your thinking. Practically speaking, we can treat opposition and challenges to our assumptions as a sandpaper metaphor: They may rub you the wrong way, and there may be a little friction, but you will come out smoother and more refined in the end.

I understand that some feel highlighting the differences associated with various groups hinders progress. I would argue, however, that the mere identification of unique attributes is not the problem. The problem lies in our uncertainty of what to do with this new awareness. That's where Inclusion Coaching and the COMMIT coaching model can help build a path forward toward a better future. They enable us to harness the power of shared awareness by encouraging people to bring their whole selves to the table while creating a new and improved space that works for everyone.

If looking for diverse feedback hasn't been part of your process to date, you have the opportunity to reshape your patterns of behavior to prioritize inclusion. You can start along this journey by choosing actions that honor the following considerations:

- + We must operate from the fundamental truth that everyone has inherent value and deserves to be treated with dignity and respect.

- + No longer should people have to give up a part of who they are to be successful or to "fit in."

- + No one demographic of people should set the standard for achievement, quality, or success, requiring that all others assimilate to their standard or set of cultural norms.

- + Women, people of color, and other marginalized groups must ensure that everyone—including white men—is engaged in inclusion efforts, and to do so, we have to confirm that they understand the meaning of their privilege and how to use it honorably.

+ When we operate from a place of truth—embracing the good, the bad, and the ugly relative to diversity—we demonstrate our collective strength.

WHAT'S IN IT FOR YOUR LIFE

In this book, I've shared some key experiences from my life, which has been a beautiful, eclectic journey filled with all kinds of people, global travels, and cultural exploration. My personal interest in learning and growing from cultural encounters has helped me in the workplace, supporting my success at multinational Fortune 500 companies throughout my career. Living my life with an eye toward learning from, connecting with, and empowering a wide spectrum of people from all walks of life, personally and professionally—as well as having compassion for and awareness of my own background and insights—has sharpened my decision-making and problem-solving skills and opened me up to some of the best moments of my life. Our existence is so much better when we get out there and embrace the opportunities and challenges that come along with living inclusively. I encourage everyone to remain curious about the treasures that lie in people unlike themselves.

NINE D&I TRUTHS

As our journey together comes to an end—and the next stage of your D&I trek begins—I want to highlight some of the key insights we've covered throughout this book. I hope you will keep in mind these nine D&I Truths as you work to develop an inclusion mind-set for yourself, your team, and your organization.

1. Human beings are primed to perform optimally when they feel seen and valued for who they truly are, and when their uniqueness is viewed as an asset, not a deficit.

2. Visible diversity in our workforces is a start, but making inclusion an embedded reality requires that we go deeper.

3. Inclusion is about creating a new space where everyone can be their authentic selves and we can all move forward together. It is not about giving up a part of ourselves, assimilating, or taking measures to fit into the dominant culture.

4. Inclusion necessitates a heartfelt change in understanding, perspective, and behavior. This shift must start with, and be modeled and supported by, those with the power to initiate change throughout the enterprise.

5. Inclusion Coaching works to move those in power beyond lip service by calling on them to explore their own truths and become curious about the needs and experiences of others. The COMMIT coaching model is the "how" of everyday inclusion.

6. Making the effort to recognize both covert and overt forms of bias and discrimination removes the veil of denial and avoidance and makes visible the problems that discrimination creates.

7. Listening deeply goes beyond accurately hearing what someone else has said; it's about the impact, the motive, and the intent.

8. Advocating for others' freedom of expression enables us to embody the fullest expression of ourselves.

9. Experiencing the full expression of employees' and colleagues' identities affords us innumerable advantages, from personal fulfillment to organizational profitability.

A CALL TO ACTION

My experiences have given me the courage to speak my truth and lean into the discomfort of addressing sensitive topics. My grandson is one of my greatest inspirations, and my sincerest hope is that his generation will reach a state of oneness and unity throughout society that mine has not yet been able to achieve.

Building on the understanding that inclusion works only when everyone takes responsibility for their part in building a culture of inclusion, here is my challenge for you:

♦ *What are the things you will take away from this book, and how will you personally put them into action?*

If any of what we've covered here has sparked the inclusion strategist within you, and you've read about something you'd like to take even further, please do. I'd love to hear about it. As you begin to incorporate Inclusion Coaching and the COMMIT model and principles into your life, your team dynamic, and your organizational culture, I hope you'll reach out and share your thoughts. We are in this together, after all.

Diversity-beyond-Lip-Service
Commitment Statement

As you set off on the next stage of your own D&I journey, use the following commitment statement to reinforce your thoughts, your actions, and—most important—your ongoing commitment to advancing diversity, equity, inclusion, and belonging in work and life:

I commit to courageous action, doing my best to cultivate an inclusive environment for myself, my team, my organization, and my industry.

I commit to opening my eyes and ears to the good, the bad, and the ugly, and to taking steps to champion the good and change the bad and ugly circumstances that hold us *all* back.

I commit to moving beyond lip service, making sure that I "walk the talk" when it comes to diversity, equity, inclusion, and belonging.

I commit to making room for controversy and conflict, with the knowledge that it is only when these moments of friction occur that we can transform and transcend together.

I commit to inviting new perspectives by seeking the insight of a diversity of voices, which *always* adds value.

I commit to telling the truth, even when it hurts, to challenge bias, remove barriers, and make meaningful progress.

Most of all, I commit to the continuous pursuit of diversity, equity, inclusion, and belonging with the goal of creating a better workplace and society for all.

COMMIT Self-Assessment: Where Are You in Your Journey?

I've created a self-assessment to help you determine your strengths and weaknesses around D&I. Go to lawanaharris.com to complete the assessment.

The real value of the self-assessment lies in what you do with your findings. Use the baseline you establish to determine the actions you will take to advance D&I.

How can you do more in the area in which you scored the highest?

Next, look at the area in which you scored the lowest. Create a plan to address just one of the items in this section. When you've accomplished that particular goal, move on to another. When it seems that all sections have been accomplished, reassess.

Creating a culture of inclusion is a continuous journey, and moving forward on this path requires ongoing evaluation, reflection, and courageous action.

NOTES

Chapter 1

1. U.S. Census Bureau, "New Census Bureau Report Analyzes U.S. Population Projections," March 3, 2015, https://www.census.gov/newsroom/press-releases/2015/cb15-tps16.html.

Chapter 2

1. Kenji Yoshino, "Covering," *Yale Law Journal* 111, no. 4 (January 2002), https://www.yalelawjournal.org/article/covering.

2. Ibid.

Chapter 3

1. Peggy McIntosh, *White Privilege and Male Privilege: A Personal Account of Coming to See Correspondences Through Work in Women's Studies* (Wellesley, MA: Wellesley College Center for Research on Women, 1988), 189.

2. https://www.diversityinc.com/diversityinc-ceo-luke-viscontis-final-remarks-at-2018-top-50-event

Chapter 4

1. Magdalena Mook, "How Coaching Can Create a Diverse and Inclusive Workplace," *Business Journals*, May 12, 2017, https://www.bizjournals.com/bizjournals/how-to/human-resources/2017/05/how-coaching-can-create-a-diverse-and-inclusive.html.

2. Madison Park, "What the Starbucks Incident Tells Us About Implicit Bias," CNN, April 17, 2018, https://www.cnn.com/2018/04/17/health/implicit-bias-philadelphia-starbucks/index.html, accessed June 15, 2018.

3. Ibid.

4. "Starbucks to Close All Stores Nationwide for Racial-Bias Education on May 29," Starbucks, April 17, 2018, https://news.starbucks.com/press-releases/starbucks-to-close-stores-nationwide-for-racial-bias-education-may-29, accessed June 19, 2018.

5. Stedman Graham, *Diversity: Leaders Not Labels* (New York: Free Press/Simon & Schuster, 2006), 224.

6. S. Barton Cutter, "Coaching for Inclusion: A Whole Person Accommodation," Careers in Government, June 4, 2016, https://www.careersingovernment.com/tools/gov-talk/career-advice/on-the-job/coaching-inclusion-whole-person-accommodation/, accessed January 18, 2018.

7. Since I am a global leadership development professional, facilitator, and trainer, you know that I have to have an acronym somewhere!

8. To explore where you are, I encourage you to go to lawanaharris.com to complete the self-assessment.

Chapter 5

1. Nancy M. Carter et al., *The Bottom Line: Corporate Performance and Women's Representation on Boards*, Catalyst, https://www.catalyst .org/knowledge/bottom-line-corporate-performance-and-womens-representation-boards.

2. Governor Edmund G. Brown Jr. of California, letter, September 30, 2018, https://www.gov.ca.gov/wp-content/uploads/2018/09/SB-826-signing-message.pdf.

3. "Who We Are," 30% Club, https://30percentclub.org/about/who-we-are.

4. "Diversity," Google, https://diversity.google.

Chapter 6

1. "CEO Action for Diversity & Inclusion™ Launches Nationwide Unconscious Bias Tour to Engage 12 Million Employees and Students," CEO Action for Diversity & Inclusion, press release, June 11, 2018, https://www.ceoaction.com/media/press-releases/2018/ceo-action-for-diversity-inclusion-launches-nationwide-unconscious-bias-tour-to-engage-12-million-employees-and-students/, accessed June 26, 2018.

2. Jonathan Soroff, "The Eyes Have It," *Improper Bostonian*, May 23, 2014, http://www.improper.com/arts-culture/the-eyes-have-it/.

3. Dina Gerdeman, "Minorities Who 'Whiten' Job Resumes Get More Interviews," Harvard Business School Working Knowledge, May 17, 2017, https://hbswk.hbs.edu/item/minorities-who-whiten-job-resumes-get-more-interviews, accessed January 18, 2018.

4. Marianne Bertrand and Sendhil Mullainathan, "Are Emily and Greg More Employable Than Lakisha and Jamal? A Field Experiment on Labor Market Discrimination," National Bureau of Economic Research, July 2003, http://www.nber.org/papers/w9873, accessed January 18, 2018.

5. Gerdeman, "Minorities Who 'Whiten' Job Resumes Get More Interviews."

6. Chimamanda Ngozi Adichie, "The Danger of a Single Story," TED Talk, YouTube, October 7, 2009, https://www.youtube.com/watch?v=D9Ihs241zeg&t=720s, accessed January 18, 2018.

7. Dina Bass and Ellen Huet, "Researchers Combat Gender and Racial Bias in Artificial Intelligence," Bloomberg News, December 4, 2017. In *The Globe and Mail*, https://www.theglobeandmail.com/report-on-business/researchers-combat-gender-and-racial-bias-in-artificial-intelligence/article37177350/.

8. Ibid.

9. Barbara Hoey and Alyssa Smilowitz, "Fiscal Year 2017 EEOC Statistics Are Here (and So Is Retaliation!)," LaborDays, January 29, 2018, https://www.labordaysblog.com/2018/01/fiscal-year-2017-eeoc-statistics-are-here-and-so-is-retaliation/, accessed June 26, 2018.

10. "EEOC Releases Fiscal Year 2016 Enforcement and Litigation Data," U.S. Equal Employment Opportunity Commission, press release, January 18, 2018, https://www1.eeoc.gov//eeoc/newsroom/release/1-18-17a.cfm?renderforprint=1, accessed August 6, 2018.

11. "Discrimination at Work: Prevalent Yet Subtle Workplace Bias Erodes Productivity and Engagement," VitalSmarts, press release, March 21, 2017, https://www.vitalsmarts.com/press/2017/03/discrimination-at-work-prevalent-yet-subtle-workplace-bias-erodes-productivity-and/, accessed January 18, 2018.

12. Ibid.

Chapter 7

1. Nao Sano and Kae Inoue, "Japan's Carmakers Have Got a Problem With Women," Bloomberg Businessweek, May 10, 2018, https://www.bloomberg.com/news/features/2018-05-10/japan-s-carmakers-have-got-a-problem-with-women, accessed June 25, 2018.

2. Tessa L. Dover, Brenda Major, and Cheryl R. Kaiser, "Members of High-Status Groups Are Threatened by Pro-Diversity Organizational Messages," *Journal of Experimental Social Psychology* 62 (January 2016), 58–67.

3. Levi Sumagaysay, "Intel Security Costs Rose After CEO, Other Execs Got Threats Over Diversity Push," *SiliconBeat, Mercury News*, April 6, 2017, http://www.siliconbeat.com/ 2017/04/06/intel-security-costs-rose-after-ceo-other-execs-got-threats-over-diversity-push/, accessed July 2, 2018.

Chapter 8

1. "Diversity & Inclusion Benchmarking Survey Global Data Sheet," PWC, https://www.pwc.com/gx/en/services/people-organisation/global-diversity-and-inclusion-survey/global-report.pdf, accessed January 18, 2018.

2. "Using Stretch Assignments to Develop Leadership Talent," SIGMA Assessment Systems, http://www.sigmaassessment systems.com/stretch-assignments/, accessed January 17, 2018.

3. The Tanenbaum Center for Interreligious Understanding, *One-Third of U.S. Employees Say Employers Do Not Accommodate Religion in Workplaces*, August 30, 2015.

4. David Marshall, "Why a 'Moment of Silence' Before BK Staff Meetings?" Berrett-Koehler Publishers, https://www.bkconnection.com/groups/ask-jeeves/conversations/why-a-moment-of-silence-before-bk-staff-meetings, accessed July 9, 2018.

5. Alison Moodie, "Are US Businesses Doing Enough to Support Religious Diversity in the Workplace?" *Guardian*, January 28, 2016, https://www.theguardian.com/sustainable-business/2016/jan/28/religious-diversity-us-business-muslim-hijab-discrimination-equal-employment-eeoc, accessed July 3, 2018.

6. Kathryn Tyler, "How to Help Middle Managers Succeed," SRHM, June 1, 2016, https://www.shrm.org/hr-today/news/hr-magazine/0616/pages/how-hr-can-help-middle-managers-succeed.aspx, accessed July 5, 2018.

Chapter 9

1. "How to Implement Positive Habits," Axtschmiede, http://axtschmiede.com/implement-positive-habits/.

2. Sara Uhlig, "Neuroplasticity—a Sentis Video," MindUp, September 21, 2017, https://mindup.org/neuroplasticity-sentis-video/.

Chapter 10

1. Quoted in Marcia Reynolds, "5 Steps for Managing Your Emotional Triggers," *Psychology Today*, July 8, 2015, https://www.psychologytoday.com/us/blog/wander-woman/201507/5-steps-managing-your-emotional-triggers.

2. Anna Johansson, "What Millennials Want in Your Inclusion Program," *Forbes*, June 26, 2017, https://www.forbes.com/sites/annajohansson/2017/06/26/what-millennials-want-in-your-inclusion-program/#7e3f36e01a07.

Chapter 11

1. Ella Louise Bell, "The Bicultural Life Experience of Career-Oriented Black Women," *Journal of Organizational Behavior* 11, no. 6 (November 1990).

2. Quoted in Sylvia Ann Hewlett, "Too Many People of Color Feel Uncomfortable at Work," *Harvard Business Review*, October 18, 2012, https://hbr.org/2012/10/too-many-people-of-color-feel.

3. Ibid.

Conclusion

1. Hoey and Smilowitz, "Fiscal Year 2017 EEOC Statistics Are Here (and So Is Retaliation)!"

2. "New Deloitte Research Identifies Keys to Creating Fair and Inclusive Organizations," *PR Newswire*, May 10, 2017, https://www.prnewswire.com/news-releases/new-deloitte-research-identifies-keys-to-creating-fair-and-inclusive-organizations-300455164.html, accessed January 18, 2018.

3. Dorie Clark, "How Diversity and Inclusion Are Driving the Bottom Line at American Express," *Forbes*, April 23, 2015, https://www.forbes.com/sites/dorieclark/2015/04/23/how-diversity-and-inclusion-are-driving-the-bottom-line-at-american-express/#f8534f3575d5, accessed August 6, 2018.

GLOSSARY

bias: Prejudices for and against various characteristics. Characteristics that frequently evoke bias include gender identity, race, ethnicity, age, sexual orientation, weight, and religion, among many others.

blind spot: An area where one's objective view is obstructed, potentially by one's bias or limited world view.

CEO Action Network: A coalition designed to bring together leaders willing to actively advance diversity and inclusion in the workplace.

Chinese New Year: A major holiday in Greater China marking the beginning of the Chinese calendar year, falling between January 21 and February 20.

color blindness: The claim that an individual—usually belonging to the dominant majority—"doesn't see race or color" when considering others, effectively minimizing experiences that differ from his or her own.

COMMIT: A six-step coaching model that helps individuals ask questions of themselves and others to build a more inclusive mind-set in work and life.

covering: Attempting to keep a stigmatized aspect of one's identity from playing a prominent role in one's interactions.

cultural competence: Respecting and reflecting the beliefs and needs of diverse groups in policies, procedures, and personal interactions.

diversity: Composing different elements. For our purposes, *diversity* refers to different types of people representing a variety of characteristics, backgrounds, and opinions.

diversity and inclusion maturity: The state in which all of an organization's diversity, equity, and inclusion mandates and goals are clearly defined and reflected in company policies, processes, and employee behaviors.

Employee Resource Groups (ERGs): Voluntary groups within an organization comprising individuals who share identity characteristics or backgrounds.

Equal Employment Opportunity Commission (EEOC): The U.S. organization responsible for enforcing federal laws that protect applicants and employees from discrimination based on race, color, religion, gender identity and sexual orientation, national origin, age, disability, or genetic information.

frozen middle: Midlevel managers who say they are on board with advancing diversity and inclusion, but who do little to nothing to advance it.

gender-neutral pronoun: A pronoun that is not associated with a particular gender. This takes the place of gendered pronouns like *him* or *her* but does not carry a male or female designation. *They* and *ze* are common gender-neutral pronouns.

hashtag: A word or phrase preceded by a hash sign (#), used to identify and link content on social media channels such as Twitter, Facebook, and Instagram.

Heritage Day: Formerly called Shaka Day, Heritage Day is a national holiday recognizing South Africa's multicultural makeup while cementing a unified future.

inclusion: Involving or accommodating all parties.

Inclusion Circles: Group meetings that serve as circles of trust for unfiltered dialogue where people can learn and grow together.

Inclusion Coaching: A coaching methodology and corresponding strategies developed by La'Wana Harris that aim to help individuals increase the inclusiveness of their organizations and their lives, achieving a better world for all.

Latinx: A person of Latin American origin or descent (Latinx is used as a gender-neutral or nonbinary alternative to Latino or Latina).

LGBTQIA: An inclusive acronym that includes the majority of gender and sexual identities—lesbian, gay, bisexual, trans, queer, intersex, and asexual.

Lunar New Year: The beginning of the year as dictated by the cycles of the moon.

melanated: Containing melanin, a brown or black pigment found in hair, skin, and eyes.

#MeToo: A movement that supports the survivors of sexual abuse, assault, and harassment.

microaggression: Subtle comment or action that demonstrates bias against an individual from a marginalized group.

millennials: Those born in the 1980s through the early 2000s, and reaching adulthood during the early-twenty-first century.

neurodiversity: Short for *neurological diversity*, *neurodiversity* refers to the rich diversity in the way that human brains and minds operate, and to the idea that this is a natural, valuable form of difference.

neuroleadership: A method developed by consultant and leadership coach David Rock that uses neuroscience findings to transform traditional leadership.

neuroplasticity: The ability of the brain to form and reorganize synaptic connections, especially in response to learning, a new experience, or a traumatic injury.

only one: The sole individual in a group or organization representing a particular characteristic or set of characteristics.

PAUSE: A model used to navigate and explore conflict and controversy.

privilege: Rights, benefits, or advantages exclusively granted to particular groups of people.

trigger: A characteristic, situation, or event that elicits a strong response based on previous experiences or beliefs.

unconscious bias: Prejudices and stereotypes for and against various characteristics formed without an individual's awareness. Characteristics that frequently evoke bias include gender identity, race, ethnicity, age, sexual orientation, weight, and religion, among many others.

woke: A political term that refers to maintaining an awareness of social and racial justice.

ACKNOWLEDGMENTS

Thank you, Eddie, my first love, my high school sweetheart, my prom date, my best friend, and my husband. For thirty-four years you have selflessly supported and encouraged me to take risks in pursuit of my passion. You've lived every second of this book with me, so it gave me strength and certainty when you said the time for my book is now. It is a privilege to do life with you.

I also want to thank my children, Eddie II, Malcolm, and Jasmine, who constantly inspire me to tap into my inner millennial. It's been so cool to have reverse mentoring from you throughout the ideation and writing process. You'd probably give me a "jargon" demerit for that last sentence.

Sincere appreciation goes to everyone who played a role in getting this book to publication—notably, my literary agent, Leticia, who helped me join the Berrett-Koehler family; and my editors, Jeevan for pushing me to go where no one has gone before, Neal for reeling me in when I wandered off the farm, and Danielle for providing valuable insights in the final stretch.

Finally, I'd like to thank everyone who has shared this journey with me through stories, tears, laughter, anger, joy, and, most important, hope. I can't list all the names, but I pray this book is evidence of my heartfelt thank-you and commitment to do something about all that we've been through together. Nothing that we've been through will be wasted.

INDEX

ABOUT THE AUTHOR

Jack Carver, Headshots Raleigh

An inspirational leader and dynamic facilitator, La'Wana Harris is a Certified Diversity Executive, an ICF Credentialed Coach, and a global leadership development professional who has dedicated her career to aligning performance with business strategy. She has demonstrated success across a broad range of corporate functions, including global leadership and organizational development, diversity and inclusion, government affairs, and market access. In addition, as a community activist she has created diversity and inclusion awareness programs and designed overall integrated management solutions.

La'Wana is driven by a firm belief in honoring and speaking the truth, no matter how challenging that may be. As a result, she's recognized throughout the leadership community as someone gifted in sparking meaningful and insightful dialogue that ultimately inspires change.

Throughout the decades of her professional career and social justice activism, La'Wana has received numerous industry and community awards. Most recently, she was recognized as one of 2018's 100 Most Inspiring People in the life-sciences industry by *PharmaVOICE* magazine. She also received the Women in Leadership award from the National Black MBA Association and was invited to join the Forbes Coaches Council as a contributor and thought leader.

La'Wana is dedicated to helping make the world a better place at work and at home. As a tireless community activist, she has spent the past twenty-seven years facilitating civic engagement and collective action at community and nonprofit organizations around the country. She is an alumna of the Leadership Greensboro and the Other Voices programs in Greensboro, North Carolina, and and has led diversity initiatives at large multinational organizations.

La'Wana is also a respected humanitarian and philanthropist. Understanding how important it is for children to read books with characters they can relate to, she created two book series featuring children of color. These books promote cultural diversity and are translated in the native languages of underserved nations. La'Wana has donated 10,000 books in Haitian Creole to schools and orphanages in partnership with Grace International. Through her efforts, U.S. sales from these books help support young females entering careers in STEM.

La'Wana and her husband have three adult children and one adorable grandson.

To learn more about La'Wana and engage in the important work of advancing diversity and inclusion, visit lawanaharris.com.

Action Guide for Diversity Beyond Lip Service

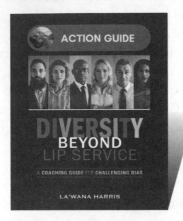

It's time to "walk the talk." The *Action Guide for Diversity Beyond Service* provides pragmatic tips for embedding inclusive behaviors throughout your organization. Share this guide with your leaders and their teams to help them develop a common baseline for daily inclusive practices.

ISBN 978-1-946388-08-7

The Inclusion Circle™ Card Deck

Knowing where to start with authentic dialogue about D&I issues can be a challenge for many leaders. The Inclusion Circle™ Card Deck is an effective tool to get meaningful conversations started in an engaging format. Empower your leaders to create nonjudgmental, safe spaces with simple instructions to allow for greater connection with intact and cross-functional teams.

Order the Inclusion Circle™ Card Deck now at lawanaharris.com.

Global Diversity & Inclusion Benchmarks

Global Diversity & Inclusion Benchmarks: Standards for Organizations Around the World (GDIB) helps organizations determine strategy and measure progress in managing diversity and fostering inclusion. It is a free downloadable eighty-page booklet that can be used by submitting a permission agreement. The GDIB was written by the Centre for Global Inclusion's founding board members, Julie O'Mara, board chair and president, and Alan Richter, PhD, treasurer, as well as ninety-five expert panelists.

centreforglobalinclusion.org

Inclusion Nudges

People in the Inclusion Nudges community empower and enable each other to increase inclusion by sharing their nudges for inclusion. This nonprofit global initiative is free for all and provides equal access for all.

inclusion-nudges.org

Berrett–Koehler
BK Publishers

Berrett-Koehler is an independent publisher dedicated to an ambitious mission: *Connecting people and ideas to create a world that works for all.*

Our publications span many formats, including print, digital, audio, and video. We also offer online resources, training, and gatherings. And we will continue expanding our products and services to advance our mission.

We believe that the solutions to the world's problems will come from all of us, working at all levels: in our society, in our organizations, and in our own lives. Our publications and resources offer pathways to creating a more just, equitable, and sustainable society. They help people make their organizations more humane, democratic, diverse, and effective (and we don't think there's any contradiction there). And they guide people in creating positive change in their own lives and aligning their personal practices with their aspirations for a better world.

And we strive to practice what we preach through what we call "The BK Way." At the core of this approach is *stewardship,* a deep sense of responsibility to administer the company for the benefit of all of our stakeholder groups, including authors, customers, employees, investors, service providers, sales partners, and the communities and environment around us. Everything we do is built around stewardship and our other core values of *quality, partnership, inclusion,* and *sustainability.*

This is why Berrett-Koehler is the first book publishing company to be both a B Corporation (a rigorous certification) and a benefit corporation (a for-profit legal status), which together require us to adhere to the highest standards for corporate, social, and environmental performance. And it is why we have instituted many pioneering practices (which you can learn about at www.bkconnection.com), including the Berrett-Koehler Constitution, the Bill of Rights and Responsibilities for BK Authors, and our unique Author Days.

We are grateful to our readers, authors, and other friends who are supporting our mission. We ask you to share with us examples of how BK publications and resources are making a difference in your lives, organizations, and communities at www.bkconnection.com/impact.

Dear reader,

Thank you for picking up this book and welcome to the worldwide BK community! You're joining a special group of people who have come together to create positive change in their lives, organizations, and communities.

What's BK all about?

Our mission is to connect people and ideas to create a world that works for all.

Why? Our communities, organizations, and lives get bogged down by old paradigms of self-interest, exclusion, hierarchy, and privilege. But we believe that can change. That's why we seek the leading experts on these challenges—and share their actionable ideas with you.

A welcome gift

To help you get started, we'd like to offer you a **free copy** of one of our bestselling ebooks:

www.bkconnection.com/welcome

When you claim your **free ebook**, you'll also be subscribed to our blog.

Our freshest insights

Access the best new tools and ideas for leaders at all levels on our blog at ideas.bkconnection.com.

Sincerely,

Your friends at Berrett-Koehler